SELFISH *Mind,* SLAVISH *Body*

SELFISH *Mind,* SLAVISH *Body*

A Quest into Self-identity

Laljee Verma

Hay House Publishers India
Australia • India
United Kingdom • United States

Hay House Publishers (India) Pvt. Ltd.
Muskaan Complex, Plot No.3, B-2 Vasant Kunj, New Delhi-110 070, India
Hay House Inc., PO Box 5100, Carlsbad, CA 92018-5100, USA
Hay House UK, Ltd., The Sixth Floor, Watson House, 54 Baker Street, W1U 7BU, UK
Hay House Australia Pty Ltd., 18/36 Ralph St., Alexandria NSW 2015, Australia

Email: contact@hayhouse.co.in
www.hayhouse.co.in

ISBN 978-93-91067-99-1
ISBN 978-93-91067-05-2 (e-book)

Printed at Repro India Limited

For my grandchildren:

Shagun, Satvik, Shobhit, and Shreyas.

May you one day find the inclination to read and enjoy this book and its contents.

Contents

Preface 9

Introduction 13

1. The Dilemma of Identity 23
   - i. Who Am I? 23
   - ii. Life Energy-Soul Relationship 36
   - iii. The Three-Element Concept 39
   - iv. Religion and Faith 45
   - v. Spirituality 67
   - vi. Genes: Deterministic of Life 86
2. Mind-Body Complex 95
   - i. Part I 95
   - ii. Part II 121
   - iii. Part III 126
3. God Delusion 159
4. I, Me, Myself 173
   - i. General Consideration 173
   - ii. Self-Centricity 179
5. In Conclusion 191

Acknowledgements 199

References 203

Bibliography and Further Reading 213
Notes 218
Index 223

Preface

MAN IS NOT INFALLIBLE. WE ALL COMMIT MISTAKES, and the results of an error can be external or internal. But a mistake may not represent the core nature of an individual. One may do something quite against his fundamental nature. In such events, the mind may not be within the control. The mind, at times, defies logic and steps out of the restraining envelop. The question then is what can control the mind? The answer is that it is the *mind* only that can control the mind. This may sound contradictory, but there is no other way.

One may wonder as to how the mind can exercise control over itself. That is precisely the point. We may ask then how can the self, exercise control over itself. The answer is that the self has many mechanisms within through which it can exercise restraint. Likewise, the mind also has a corrective tool through which it can exercise self-control. As in the God-concept, we have a god and an anti-god competing. Similarly, in our mind, virtuous and sinful thoughts continuously compete with each other. The outcome of an action will depend upon which of these two elements dominate at a particular time and space. No doubt, restraining mechanisms such as rationality and logic does exist in our mind, but it may fail, or purposely allowed to fail, at times. And when the virtuous element fails, the sinful element dominates, resulting in an undesirable act. Sinful actions may provide momentary pleasure, but the fun may quickly transform into a continuous painful memory of having committed a sinful activity transgressing the logical boundary. Pleasure and joy are different states of feeling. Pleasure is momentary, whereas joy is long-lasting and durable. Most of us look for pleasure, not joy. Only a few go after joy, and very few aspire to experience everlasting joy.

Sometimes, under the emotive influence, we do something quite against our basic nature. During such cases, we willingly let go of the restraint over our mind. The ego, and its soldiers—lust, greed, envy, etc.—acquire demonic proportion and subdue the rationality. That is when we commit acts which should have never happened. This is the story of many. No one in the world is free from ego, lust, and greed. When such forces take over, it is a natural tendency to veer towards sin. And once such a thing happens, only then one realises that he does not know himself and his mind. If one does not fight a faulty experience and put a restraint over his mind, one becomes a slave of his ego. The mind is selfish, it does not like to be restrained; it tries to lord over the body as its slave. But unrestrained mind is a devil's warehouse hoarding sinful thoughts, and therefore, one must master the mind and not be its slave. It is therefore necessary to identify it. Only then a corrective action can be applied. But for this, one must be ruthlessly objective.

Everyone grows up oblivious of the correct worldview because our subjective mind determines the cognised outcome of what we see and perceive. Most of us lack objectivity. That is why each of us has a different worldview. Each person's mind is different, and therefore, the worldview of each person will be different. The actual world may be quite different than conceived with our individuated mind. Moreover, individual mind matures in stages of physical development. The worldview of a child is full of awe, inquisitiveness, and admiration, and his mind is much more curious. He wants to gather as many experiences as he can. But with time, his mind conditions itself to existential experience and conformity of social norms and ethos. As the child grows to a young adult, he sees the world as a challenge and when he grows old, he wonders about the world engulfed in the remarkable divine contribution that makes us walk and talk! However, at all these stages, the doubt about our *true self* keeps lurking. And truthfully, we all keep revisiting the quintessential question: who am I?

The mind is an essential ingredient of the self. We may perceive it as an object, gross or abstract, with sense organs but there is no way we can conceive it without involving our mind. If we do not know our mind, its peculiarities, predilection, bias, etc., our feelings and actions will remain individualistic, and heavily biased within the peculiar individual mental construct.

Knowing the self is nothing else but self-realisation. It is a state difficult to achieve as most of us like to live within the ramparts of ego and self-aggrandisement. Subjectivity prevents us from realising the self. It is difficult for anyone to be totally objective, all the time. At the same time, it is not possible to achieve an objective standpoint unless we are severely critical of ourselves. Every action has two parts: the 'why' and the 'how'. When we look back, we recapitulate the how part but do not know the why part. Therefore, we know what we did, but not why we did it!

I kept wondering day in and day out that why we do not know ourselves. What is the impenetrable screen limiting our vision to see within ourselves? What is the barrier between me and my mind? That is when I decided to research the issue. The result of two years of research and contemplation is this book in which I attempt to dismantle the mystery of the self and the mind.

Through this book, I examine various factors that determine the qualia of an individual, his nature, and his mind, and I have tried to lay bare the individuality and self-centricity that prevents us from knowing the self.

Introduction

"Know then thyself, presume not God to scan,
the proper study of mankind is man."
— Alexander Pope

THE MOST FAMOUS MAXIM 'KNOW THYSELF' IS CARVED IN the temple of Apollo at Delphi. The oracle was famous in ancient Greece. Kings, leaders, and philosophers regularly visited personally or through an envoy or messengers to seek answers to critical issues. It is said that the oracle always gave correct prophecy till the Lydian King Croesus wanted an answer to the lurking doubt whether to cross the Halys River, the boundary with the Persian Empire, and attack the forces of Cyrus the Great. The famous reply he received was that if he crossed the river, a great empire would be demolished. He took it for granted that the Persian empire and not the Lydian would be one to get demolished. Thus, he crossed the river and attacked the forces of Cyrus the Great. Though superior in number, his army lost the battle (Battle of Thymbra, 546 BC), the capital Sardis was taken, and Lydia became a satrapy of the Persian Empire. The oracle lost its prime glory, but the priests defended saying that King Croesus misinterpreted the prophecy.

You may be wondering what may be the purpose of narrating this historical piece in such a book. But then what could be the purpose of etching the famous maxim 'know thyself' in the Oracle of Delphi where people inquired prophecies? And what could be the connection between the oracle and the maxim? The answer to this question is 'subjectivity of the mind'. The oracle gave an answer to King Croesus, but he interpreted it to his liking, in accordance with his subjective mind. His mind construed the meaning which favoured his thinking. Therefore, there is a purpose in its narration. Most of us interpret indications and signs that suite our thinking, and further action is largely determined by the inherently biased subjective mind. This is not to say that our mind is always subjective, but mostly it is. A balance between subjectivity and objectivity is required to gather true impressions. Knowing outside objects and forming a biased or unbiased opinion is based on one's mental construct and attitude. And our mental status is never constant; it keeps changing with time and space. Therefore, it is necessary to know the mind every time and in every situation.

Peeping within one's own personality is difficult, just as the eyes can see without but not within. The beauty or ugliness of an object is known by the involvement of the mind and not only by the eyes, as eyes are only a sense organ for the acquisition of visual cues. Perception can be external, but conception is internal. External perception is about sensory inputs, whereas the internal ones are about ideas and thoughts that generate within the mind. Perception is an external phenomenon, whereas conception is inclusive of what the mind thinks of the object. In other words, the development of a feeling may not necessarily be in accordance with the inherent property of the object. The mental attitude of the observer at the given time and place will primarily determine its beauty, ugliness, importance, usefulness, etc. For example, if a person is hungry, the appearance of an edible fruit would appear attractive. On the other hand, the mind may just discard the image of a fruit as irrelevant if your stomach is full. "In the Nyaya theory, perception, external or internal, is reliable unless countermanded by another perception or some other evidence."[1]

Imageries pass through stages, such as object perception, impression, development of an idea, imagination, and effectual outcome. C. G. Jung (1875-1961 CE), the Swiss psychiatrist and psychoanalyst, beautifully summarises: "The psyche and its structure are real enough. They even transform material objects in psychic images, as we have said. They do not perceive waves but sound; not wavelengths, but colours."[2] The outcome may be an action or construction of an abstract idea, influenced and moderated by individual predilection. It will vary as per the degree of subjectivity or objectivity of a mind. The external stimulus (perception) experienced by sense organs, and the nature of the individual mind, both intermingle and then only a final conception emerges.

Individual psyche varies from individual to individual. Most people confuse self-knowledge with the knowledge of their conscious ego. "Anyone who has any ego-consciousness at all takes it for granted that he knows himself. But the ego knows only its own contents, not the unconscious and its contents."[3] The mind always associates ideas and develops unique inert or dynamic feelings on an object. Feelings not requiring a physical action are retained in the mind, whereas dynamic feelings require to be physically actioned. The uniqueness of feelings comes from the uniqueness of the individual mind. Object remaining the same, the variable factor is the individual mind. It is different in different individuals and different in the same individual at different time and place. Mental construct is not a permanent feature but keeps changing throughout the life modulated within the framework of time and space. Baruch Spinoza sums it explicitly in his letter to Hugo Boxel (1674 AD), "Beauty, my dear sir, is not so much of the quality of the object beheld, as an effect in him who beholds it."[4] He further asserts, "As the tastes differ, so do minds. This shows clearly enough that men judge things according to the disposition of their minds."[5] Thus, the mental construct is rather important in object conception.

The building blocks of our mental construct are the day-to-day experiences, sermons, teachings, and indoctrination received from parents and elders during childhood. This can be seen in the case of parents of school-going children where they experience how the child reveres his or her teacher and does not readily accept the teacher's mistake even if there is one. That is because the child thinks the teacher to be the last word on the subject. The child has been exposed to a new thing, new idea, or a new matter and holds the teacher in awe. Therefore, teachers play a dominant role in shaping the mind (mental development) and personality of a child. However, it is important to appreciate that a teacher must not only drill the curriculum in a child but help in all-around development of a child's psyche and personality.

Not only didactic education but religious indoctrination also cast a strong influence on the mental construct of a child. Religion, faith, and culture are influential in the making of an attitude-a mental ingredient, and incentives are provided not only by the parents and family but also by teachers, schoolmates, peer group, and the society. In the words of C. G. Jung "... the human psyche is not a self-contained and wholly individual phenomenon, but also a collective one."[6] Mental construct or the mind is the fountainhead of outlook, habit, predilection, etc., in a child or an adult. You follow a religious practice as others do, you go to a temple etc., as others do. That is the mental construct engineered by the collective psyche.

Personality has two aspects: how a person appears to others externally and the vast hinterland of internal personality hidden from outside and unknown to even oneself. This internal personality always tries to overawe the external but cannot succeed wholly as a person is, after all, bound by social norms and ethos. So, he wears a persona, a mask to hide his true feelings. Much literature is available on personality, but in simple terms, personality can be defined as the individuality of a person. Every individual is unique with distinctive anatomical, physiological, and psychological attributes. Some consult soothsayers to find out how they can improve their destiny by adding or subtracting letters from their names. Names also depict the uniqueness of a person, but to make it even more unique, people insert or omit a letter. We also keep adding peculiarities to our uniqueness by inculcating peculiar habit, idiosyncrasies, or traits. Enduring characteristics and traits modulate behaviour, mental outlook, emotions, etc. throughout the life of a person.

Individual's mind is singular and not a carbon copy. Man is not a robot with robotic behaviour. If a man were a robot, all would develop the same perceptive imprints and outcome. However, we all know that it is not so. Nature of two individuals is not the same and therefore, different persons exhibit different reactions to the same input. The human body is governed by unique genetic, physiological and psychological attributes. Thus, it is a natural corollary that mental construct also will be different in different individuals. The genetic factor is only one of the composite factors; others being the society, peer group, and environment. All these play a role in the building of a personality, and none of these can be said to be the sole determinant. Man is a social animal and retains a close interconnection within the society.

A personality is influenced and impacted by the society, by its norms and limitations, its traditions, and the societal culture. An individual and society are always at conflict. Individual freedom remains suppressed under social norms and limitations. Man tries to preserve his unique identity but being a social animal must adjust with the societal norms and limitations. Thus, his external behaviour may be at variance to what he suppresses within. If the man was so constituted that he may desire nothing more than what was designated, and abide by the true morality and ethics, there might not have been any need to impose restrictions and laws to regulate his actions. But it is not so, as people always try to transgress the social norms that bind individual freedom. Rules and laws are regularly fractured. In the words of Carl Jung, "The growth of culture consists as we know, in the progressive subjugation the animal in man. Too much of the animal distorts the civilised man, too much civilisation makes sick animals."7

Many of the societal and environmental impressions get fossilised, and these unobtrusively influence the mental makeup, thinking and physical activities. Therefore, how a person perceives an external cue and acts on it will largely depend upon his in-built personality.

Every action starts in the mind. We may know about the reasoned thought process in most cases but there are instances where one may not be able to identify the thought process. If a person does something stupid or atrocious against his fundamental nature, he may say that he had lost his mind momentarily. When pressed, he may be unable to offer any other explanation for his actions. He may not be able to pinpoint but the actual cause might be a result of some kind of repressed emotion surfacing in impulsive behaviour. Impulsive behaviour is a result of emotive build-up and appears as sparks in our mind leading to instantaneous rational or irrational behaviour. The conscious mind may not be able to discern and identify the logic or the rationale behind many of our actions. Though mankind is endowed with rational thinking, irrational actions happen often. The outcome will largely depend upon the mental maturity.

* * *

It may be noted that mental development is incremental and unique with biological development. Individuals are endowed with unique mental attitude. It is evident that there are different types of people in the world. Some neither know themselves, not others, some may know other's but not their own mind, and there are very few who may know their own as well as the mind of others. People in the third category are obviously more successful than the first two categories. Subject-object relationship and relativism is a complex phenomenon, and to know oneself one needs to have at least a basic understanding of how the mind works. Therefore, you must know your mind in the process of cognition. Mind you, knowing the mind is purely individualistic. Therefore, any effort to understand it will have to be individualistic. No teacher, no preacher, and no syllabus will tell you how to know yourself; it has to be yourself!

Let me assure you that knowing the 'Self' is elusive. It is not simple to decipher the hieroglyphs in a personality despite extensive knowledge about genes and epigenetic influences we possess today. The brain-mind complex is a vast arena of improbable, a vast football field where different players are always trying to shoot a self-goal; and the goalkeeper is the superego or the individual conscience. Most of our sinful thoughts and actions get filtered, but many get past and succeed in achieving a self-goal. One must remember that not only pious but sinful thoughts also appear in the human mind. Man is a sum-total of his own thoughts and actions. Just to entertain good thoughts and eject all evil thoughts is impossible. Fyodor Dostoevsky (1821-1881) says it beautifully in his book, *The Brothers Karamazov*, "God and Devil are fighting there and the battlefield is the heart of man"[8] We cannot keep the evil thoughts from coming, but we can always exercise restraint. The only way is to ignore or forget them. However, that may be easier said than done. Therefore, restraining the mind, to keep it under a constant check is the only way. Here I would like to quote from the TV serial, *Mahabharata*, where Lord Krishna tells Arjuna "Man is his own friend and his own enemy." To know the self the need is to bask in the brilliance of the 'friend' and move away from the dark clouds of the 'enemy' in you.

In every field, there are experts and non-experts, and people who do not fall in either. Of course, teachers and experts have gathered vast knowledge on the subject, that is how they teach. However, they remain ensnared in their own knowledge web, a bit divorced from the collective ignorance and concern of the masses. And, in my opinion, a generalist viewpoint may align more closely with the common people. I do not claim to be an expert on the subject discussed, but I have tried to find the 'self' for the general reader from the standpoint of common-sense practicality. And, most importantly, I recapitulate the old adage "A seeker after truth must doubt everything he can doubt."

The book contains four main chapters and in the chapter, 'The Dilemma of Identity', I argue that three elements constitute a life, the body, the soul, and the life energy, and not the two commonly accepted elements, the body and the soul. Religious impact on the mind also has been discussed in this chapter. In the next chapter, 'Mind-Body Complex', you will find a detailed discussion on the individual mind, its layers, and its substrates. The connecting bond between the mind and the body has evaded scientific explanation through centuries. You will find a detailed discussion on this aspect, including hypothetical considerations. God-concept is an idea deeply rooted and casts deep and indelible mark on the human mind. No one has seen God; it is only experiential. The chapter 'God Delusion' discusses the delusionary concept of God imbued in human mind. In the chapter, 'I, Me and Myself' one will find the crucial part of the discussion, the essence of the book; the inherent self-centricity which prevents to realise the Self. Nature of a self-centric person has been highlighted with suggestions on how to understand and deal with a self-centric person.

Different colours and hues remain hidden behind individual personalities, like different colours hidden within the sun's rays. One needs a prism to see these different colours. Similarly, one needs to acquire a mental prism to know what kind of a person he or she may be. Despite the vast knowledge humanity has gathered in the last few centuries through science, one may not know why an action, good or bad was started and accomplished at a given point in time, even if it was not in accordance with his or her core nature. That is where this discussion is relevant, and once again, humanity may be required to etch the maxim 'Know Thyself' on its mental plate. One needs to turn the doorknob to open the gate to self-knowledge and wisdom!

— Laljee Verma

1
The Dilemma of Identity

"He who knows others is wise; he who knows oneself is enlightened!"
— Lao Tzu

i. Who Am I?

Who am I? Every human mind is saddled with this question and continuously works to find an answer. The man may have advanced leaps and bounds in the temporal world but still does not know who he is, where he has come from, and what is his purpose. Rational inquiry has helped mankind to unravel the mystery of the creation to some extent but much of it still remains a puzzle. When such questions come to my mind, as it must, I look at myself and surmise that there must be something more in this anatomical body as the anatomy of a body is the same, whether alive or dead. Evidently, I have a body, a mind, resident life energy, and a soul within me. That is the maximum I can decipher about myself first-hand. But I also know that answers to questions like how a self is made, how a mind is constructed, why two individuals are different in every aspect, including their mental makeup, etc., can be discovered through insightful discussion.

Pristine Mind of a Child

An infant's mind is a clean slate though it may carry instinctive and intuitive experiences from its past lives. The I-ness in a child normally takes birth around four to six years of age. Thereafter, whatever the child may do or learn, is always enveloped within the cloudy shadow of his self-ego, and associated features that come with ego, that is desire, envy, possessiveness etc. It is true that a child's development may be influenced by parental and environmental factors, but the I-ness plays a vital role in the later development of his personality. Generally, a child believes blindly in whatever he is told and does not feel the necessity of verifying whatever he learns. His mind is not yet illumined with direct experience or with logic and reasoning. As the child grows, the blindly trusting nature changes, and he starts questioning everything told to him and whatever he gains by direct experience. With further growth, one acquires the ability to analyse things. As the child grows intellectual part evolves, and he seeks intellectual verification of whatever he may have learnt during early childhood.

A child is born with complete innocence and its mind is pristine, free from impressions of the material world. It is like a brand-new computer that needs to be programmed and these inputs come from the parents, religious indoctrination, peer group, and other environmental factors. Many things told by the parents appear as the gospel truth to the child. Parents, not necessarily only teach good but also bad things to their children so that the child may face the world as it comes. That is why they try and inculcate their own worldview on the formative mind of the child. The unpolluted mind of a child is a perfect target for etching misinformation and falsity that prevails in human society. All such indoctrinations, good or bad, are a precursor to the mental makeup of the child. In other words, the parent's behaviour is the cultural gift to the child. Some think that a father can be a good provider with money only, little forgetting that to inculcate human values in a child is more rewarding. If an infant could write, he may ink his thoughts as:

"I am a new-born infant. When my brain starts to grow, I reminisce my past. But what past? My bygone lives? Yes, that is it. But I cannot bring it to the fore. But if this is a virtual world, what was that I left behind? Am I only an anatomical object which can be put on a dissecting table and cut open with a scalpel to unravel the secrets of life? If life is an external admixture, where does it come from and where does it go? True, the living body is a complex phenomenon, a unification of cosmic and terrestrial energy, the fusion of *purusha* and *prakriti*. But in the absence of cosmic energy, I truly am only a lump of clay. My parents feel that they own me. That is a ludicrous assertion, a grievous error in their understanding. No one owns me wholly. Sense of owning a property comes from ego. For example, we think we own our body, but we forget that nature and cosmos with their multifactorial gifts make and sustain a living body. Sense of possessiveness is a strong attribute in human nature. Right from the body to the land and money that one owns. They consider me a property. Even if that's the case, this property is not wholly owned by individual parents, not even by any single terrestrial or cosmic source. This property has many stakeholders. Nature has a stake in me. Plants, air, sun, and moon, all have a stake. These own a share in the property. No one can claim exclusive rights, not even the Almighty, since without nature, cosmic or life energy alone cannot construct an anatomical and physiological object and without cosmic energy, nature cannot exist."

Thus, we see two things: one is that the mind of a new-born child is a clean slate and free from all the terrestrial impressions of the empirical world, and two that a child may not be an object wholly owned by the parents. When he grows up, he acquires an individuality of his own.

Adult Mind

That is as far as the growing mind of a child is concerned. But even adults present mental attitude difficult to understand. What one may have gathered in the process of growing up, education, experiences, etc., all converge into a personality. However, knowing a personality is not complete until one also gathers what lies in his mind. After all, personality projection of a person is an extension of his mind. Man's behaviour is in accordance with his mental makeup. Generally, one is aware of his conscious mind but not his subconscious or the ontology and epistemology of his thoughts. Unless one knows what secrets lie in his subconscious, his inward and outward behaviour may not be in tune with his whole personality. And a person who does not have any connection with his subconscious is more likely to be self-centred. He may develop a disdainful attitude towards the world and the environment. As for the inner personality, it very much depends upon what one draws from his subconscious and how critical and objective he is towards himself. All this will be factored into the making of a personality. Action or reaction to an outward object or an incident will thus be in accordance with what the mind thinks with his conscious awareness.

Conscious awareness is only the front of the mirror. At the back is the vast hinterland of the subconscious. The subconscious needs to be brought to the fore to have a composite view. The process of individuation is both psychic and physical. The psychic aspect involves drawing ideas, feelings, the sunken physicalism, and empiricism out from the subconscious, and the physical aspect involves adjusting, modulating, and moderating the way he appears with the involvement of his conscious mind. But it is not so easy to grasp the underlying workings of the subconscious which is an abstract phenomenon. It is easy to capture gross but not the abstract. And, when discussing the self, obviously abstract phenomena such as the mind, soul, and life energy need to be examined and known. Life is a composite phenomenal development of all these things. Unless we know what life is in its compositeness, we cannot know ourselves because life is an essential part of the self. Nothing is more mysterious than life itself. When we try to unravel the mystery of life, we encounter a barrier beyond which we know lies the secret of life but are unable to see or perceive it. The secret of life remains out of grasp. Adam ate the fruit from the tree of knowledge but was not allowed to eat the fruit from the tree of life. Human beings acquired rationality through knowledge but remained ignorant about the force of life or life energy. Knowledge about life energy continues to remain distinct from the knowledge computed by human wisdom. Any amount of knowledge and wisdom that humanity has gained through scientific exploration has failed to open the first page of life energy.

Sustaining the Living Body

The primary feature of a living species is to sustain life and procreate. And for this, naturally, the body will need to be nourished. These two features are dominantly evident. On further evolution, we find mobility developing in animals and finally, features of discernment and rationality arising in the human mind. As per the Indian Vedanta philosophy and Upanishads, *atman* is within the *panch kosha* (five sheaths or coverings). The *Annamaya kosha* relates to the vegetative energy for the physical body, the *Pranamaya kosha* relates to the assimilation of food into life energy, the *Manomaya kosha* relates to the development of the inner self, the *Vijnanamaya kosha* relates to the development of wisdom, and the *Anandamaya kosha* relates to the blissful state where one realises *atman* or the self (see Fig 1).

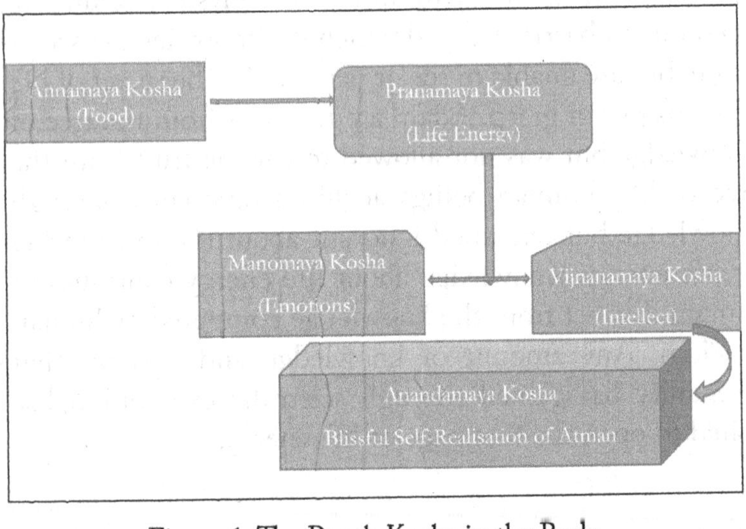

Figure 1: The Panch Kosha in the Body

Let us look at it with a more detailed explanation. *Anna* or food is essential for life, but it must be converted to useful life energy, i.e., the *Pranamaya kosha.* Once life energy is gained, the body develops ego, desire, and emotions, which is the *Manomaya kosha.* Emotions determine different physiological, behavioural, and cognitive changes; we may call these as the emotional construct. Emotions result in physical and psychological changes that influence our behaviour. Our outward behaviour and mood follow our emotional construct. After *Manomaya kosha* is the *Vijnanamaya kosha,* the layer concerned with intellect, wisdom, and ability to discern. It is here that emotions come face-to-face with intellect and discernment. Emotions are checked to obtain a state of balanced behaviour. Some may succeed in checking the emotional outburst, some may not, but the intellectual layer does try to mitigate the severity of emotions. And then lastly, the *Anandamaya kosha,* the blissful state of self-realisation, where one may realise the inner self or *atman.* The biological pattern is obvious in this entire process. First, the food, then energy from food, then the emotional construct and the intelligence, and finally, realising the self. Steps to sustain a body eventually is aimed at reaching the blissful state of self realisation. In true sense realising the soul is realising the self.

Mortal or Immortal Soul

Many philosophers have tried to deal with the question that whether the soul is mortal or immortal. Also, if the soul only pertains to human beings or whether animals have it as well. Western philosophers, such as Rene Descartes (1596-1650 AD), considered animals as machines without soul, meaning thereby that though they are living species, they do not have a soul. Arguably, what Descartes hypothesised that animals are machines without soul (mind) does not stand on logic and rationality. He may have meant that animals do not have a language and therefore, do not have a mind. But that is incorrect as animals are known to communicate. They are known to utter warning sounds, mating calls, etc. They cannot, therefore, be said to possess no language. Not to understand their language is a human failing, it does not signify its absence among animals. Language is a result of mind; not that mind is dependent on language. After all, what is language? Language is a means of communication. Some tribes know the human language but prefer to correspond with whistling sound as it travels far and wide in the valleys, like people on the Canary Islands.[9] They are known to ask a question and receive answers through different whistle sounds by twisting their lips and tongue, positioning, and repositioning their fingers inserted in their mouth. In fact, *Sylbo Gomero,* the language of whistling sound, was on the decline but stands revived with UNESCO support since 2009, and now it is taught in schools on the island. The spoken sound may travel up to about a km at the maximum. In contrast, whistling sound travels 3-4 km and is especially useful in hilly terrain. Its use had declined with world-wise use of cell phones, but now it stands revived as a heritage language.

One thing stands out in the Cartesian philosophy that life energy and soul (or the mind) are different entities, as he proposes and says that animals are machines without soul. It will appear logical only if we concede to the postulate that a soul is different from life energy because life energy is obviously present in all living species immaterial to whether they have a soul or not. As against this, other ancient religions such as Hinduism and Jainism maintain that all living things, from the smallest to the largest, are also souls with a body. But the fact remains that with all the wisdom and knowledge, we still remain in the dark about the epistemology of a soul. We also do not know for certain if the soul and the mind are the same or whether a soul is synonymous with life energy. Mankind remains somewhat ignorant of the true nature of the soul. Most religions in the world believe that a soul is an extension of the Almighty. It is true that different religions name and understand the Almighty differently, but the essence of the interrelatedness between a soul and the Almighty remains the same—the soul is a part of the Almighty temporarily residing with a body. (It may be noted here that soul may not be an integral part of a body, wholly residing within. That is why I say, 'with a body' and not 'in a body'). Religious discourses, however, remain entirely hypothetical. The true nature and feature of the soul and the Almighty remain out of grasp to human understanding.

* * *

Moses was not allowed to see the face of God but only His back when He passed through. Naming the God is forbidden in Judaism, Islam professes a faceless Allah, and followers of Sanatana Dharma, the ancient Hindu religion, consider Brahman to be the ultimate truth which cannot be known through a human mind. There is saying that it is not possible to know the knower of knowing. Therefore, by design, humanity remains in the dark about the ultimate truth and the abstract phenomena remain wrapped in a nimbus. And when rationality fails, religion and spirituality come in to fill the void. But in this guesswork, numerous doctrines—what we call religion—

develop. All such doctrines only end up circumscribing the human mind and don't have much success to get humanity anywhere nearer to the ultimate truth. Ultimate truth is the centre-point of universal consciousness and sincere dedication and perseverance are required to walk along the road of true spirituality. Many believe that to get into the spiritual endeavour, one has to distance himself from materialism. That is one of the reasons many people want to progress in spirituality through religion and religious teachings, whereas to climb the ladder of true spirituality, one needs to effect a change in his mentation and outlook. As stated, the human mind contains a combination of sinful and virtuous thoughts. It is necessary to draw upon the good aspect of man's nature and suppress the sinful attributes. It cannot be achieved till we live with the idea of a sectarian God-concept, monotheistic or polytheistic. One may or may not be deeply religious but if he harbours ill-feeling towards another individual, another species, another religion, another set of people, he is bound to miss on the good points of every religion. After all, religion has a purpose in life which is to attain a higher existential platform.

* * *

Many philosophers also equate the mind as the soul. And on deeper analysis, there appears a similarity between soul and mind. Both are abstract and may or may not be residing wholly within a body. In case they fully reside within the body, then it implies that they get destroyed upon death like heart and spleen. If they are not a part of the body, then how does the mind activate action thoughts that arise in the mental frame? The philosophical and the metaphysical view is that the mind and soul are abstract attributes of a living object impacting its functionality, but they do not completely reside within a living body. A living body is like a doll under remote control. We all must have seen a puppet show. In it, the puppeteer sits on a higher platform unseen by the audience and performs with various dolls on the stage. Puppet and puppeteer are bound together with a thread through which the puppeteer makes the puppet act and dance. If the thread is severed, the puppets become inactive, losing their lively features, even though the puppeteer is still there. Also, the demonstrated impact of the puppeteer is felt only till the doll is there and if there is no doll, there is no impact. Similarly, the impact of the mind and soul is felt only until the body is alive. If there is no life, one cannot see, feel, and experience their impact. Upon death, mind and the soul leave a dead body but remain existent somewhere in the time-space continuum. Thus, we may conclude that the mind and soul cannot be a resident part of the living body. No doubt, they are immanent part of a living body but are not its integral part. Since we are not fully knowledgeable about the true nature of the soul, we may consider the following postulates:

1. Upon death, the soul, being a part of the Almighty, merges with Him.
2. If it is a part of the cosmic energy, it must dissolve in its sparkling embrace.
3. The individual mind must find its resting place back into the lap of the universal mind.
4. If it is individual consciousness, it will merge with cosmic consciousness.

Thus, after death, each ingredient of a living body goes back to where it came from; ethereal components to the cosmos and the earthly elements to the earth and nature. In his book, *Meditations on First Philosophy*, first published in 1641 CE in Latin, Rene Descartes supports this view and says, "... although I do certainly possess a body, ... in so far as it is only an extended and unthinking thing, it is certain that I [that is, my mind, by which I am what I am] is entirely and truly distinct from my body, and may exist without it."[10]

Philosophers in ancient India and Greece, as well as many philosophers and scientists in the current era, have spent immense time and energy trying to unravel the mysteries of the mind and body relation, but without any groundbreaking success. Science may have advanced, but the final veil over the riddle is still to be lifted and the answer remains as elusive as it was.

Thought to Action

All bodily activity starts with a thought generated in the mind. Thought to a decision and action is accomplished by the mutual workings of the mind and body. Thoughts are generated in the mental vault, and the action is accomplished through the body. Effects are experienced by the body as well as the mind. If it is a somatic action, the effect is mainly felt by the body. You may punch hard and fracture some of the metacarpal bones. You might suffer a bodily injury but the pain will be felt in your mind. If you win an argument, berate a person you love, or if someone else does the same to you, your mind will feel the pleasure, pain, and grief, accordingly. It will purely be a mental experience and not corporeal. Of course, in the long run, mental worry can affect the body, but the instantaneous effect in such cases is limited to a feeling.

Now, let us get back to the thought to action discussion. Physical actions end in causing physical changes in the target object. Some actions are straightforward, like picking up a glass of water when you are thirsty. The body gets rid of the thirst, and the mind feels satiated. But searching for water in a desert is quite a different ball game; the mentation and activities will be quite different. Moving towards a mirage will only result in more and more thirst. Therefore, a person has to apply his experience, knowledge, and wisdom to perform a complicated task. Experience and knowledge lead to wisdom, but the uptake of knowledge and experience is influenced by individual mental make-up, thus making the emotional construct, tendency, and predilection uniquely individual. An uninformed person will still move towards a mirage, whereas a wise man will see through the façade. So, in these cases, the pathway to accomplishment is not that straightforward. People having an objective mind may select a clearer pathway, but some, with subjective mindset, may get entangled in the mesh of prevarication. Unique mental outlook, emotional construct, and behavioural patterns are prominent factors which influence determining a course of action.

And we hardly know how life energy determines a feeling to cause an effect and what is the connection between the mind and brain. Science, as well as religion, have failed to solve this riddle. It is, therefore, natural for the human mind to examine the issue on the metaphysical scale, but nothing has been revealed to satisfy the query. Over and above, our rational mind refuses to accept anything not proven objectivity-either physically or metaphysically. It is a natural human tendency. And unless we try to better understand life energy, the soul, and of course, the body, it may be impossible to know the true self. And, in this quest, it is essential to be forthright, objective, and truthful.

ii. Life Energy-Soul Relationship

Life Energy: A Part of Cosmic Energy

We all know that a living being is a combination of life energy and earthly elements. The greatest challenge is to explore what is the connection between the body and life energy—the primaeval energy that endows life in a mind-body frame. We all are quite familiar with what comprises the earthly elements but not life energy. One may say that life energy is nothing but a variant of cosmic energy. That may be true. However, when the cosmic energy conjugates with earthly ingredients generating life it has to be understood separately. Therefore, it is necessary to focus on the life energy rather on cosmic energy, as cosmic energy is also present in non-living species. That is why one needs to distinguish and separately identify the *avatar* of cosmic energy, the life energy present in living species capable of germinating life. Moreover, cosmic energy by itself cannot sprout life. It can manifest life only in conjugation with matter, just like the sun's rays can generate heat only when it strikes a physical object otherwise, it just darts across space. It is all dark grey in the deep space though it is the domain of infinite energy. Electricity can give visible light only when it is made to pass through a filament. Mind you a filament acts as a resistance, a barrier to the free flow of the electric current. Energy has to confront resistance to manifest. It needs to be arrested. No doubt, Cosmic energy (manifested part of cosmic consciousness) in the universe is vast and uncountable. Its quantum does not decrease even when we find its presence in numerous forms in nature, animate and inanimate. Even if a part of it is utilised as life energy it makes no difference to the quantum of universal cosmic energy, it records no decrease. To appreciate the vastness of cosmic energy one must understand that nature is not only the beautiful garden on the earth but the whole universe. To explain it further, every individual possesses life energy (part of cosmic energy). With the population explosion, one would expect that the cosmic energy vault will empty one day. But that may not happen, ever. It has remained the same as it was over a billion years of cosmic existence. We cannot evaluate the quantum of cosmic energy injected in the living species separately as inanimate mass and matter also contain energy, which is a part of the same vault of cosmic energy.

Cosmic energy has a unique distributional system. Positive energy is the manifested part, but there is a vast ocean of negative or dark energy that sustains the universe. Dark energy perpetually remains thirsty of full manifestation, and this unfulfilled desire of the cosmic consciousness is what sustains the universe and thus, creation goes on and on. Hypothetically, one can conjecture that there is a cosmic equation between energy quanta and mass and matter. One can put the manifest and dark energy (including vacuum energy) on the left side and the energy content in mass and matter on the right side. The equation remains unstable; the left side of the equation will always have a higher value than the right side. The manifest universe contains only a tiny part of cosmic energy. The day all cosmic energy, including the dark energy is used, perhaps the universe will collapse!

Soul: Different Concepts

Different religions conceptualise a soul differently. As discussed earlier, volumes have been written to decipher and describe the nature of soul, but no clear picture has emerged throughout the philosophical or metaphysical history of humankind. Irresistibly, a question that arises is whether the soul is synonymous with life energy or are these two essentials different. The fundamental difference between the two is that life energy does not carry a bag whereas the soul carries the bag of karma on its back. Aristotle (384-322 BCE), in the treatise, *On the Soul*, described three types of soul: the vegetative (plants), the sensitive (animals), and the rational (human beings).[11] On the other hand, Judaism and Islam consider five to seven types or features of soul. It is said that all the different types reside in a human body or the human mind and the dominance of one at a particular moment will determine man's thought and action. The crux of the matter is that all such subdivisional attributes of a soul are its qualia. The soul is one and doesn't have distinct types. What was described as different types are only the nature or the quality of a soul, just like the same way we typify individuals as optimistic, pessimistic, gregarious, overconfident, etc. It is the individual nature that is different, not individuals. Different features are qualia of human nature. Thereby meaning that we, as individuals, cannot be separately typified as vegetative, sensitive, and rational. We all harbour a soul with its qualities and these different qualities of the soul are resident in human nature all the time.

The Hindus call this idea of impressions on the soul as karma. In Jain theology, the karmic effects are said to be the *pudgal*, which are exceedingly small particles. So small that they can be perceived as matters without mass and are attached to the soul. It is like an apparel one wears and changes every day. It collects dust and one requires to wash it before wearing it again. And though the philosophy of karma is not accepted in Christianity and Islam, the doctrine of resurrection and attribution to heaven or hell clearly accepts the value of life experiences (karma) based on which God or Allah decides the soul's final abode. All this implies that it is the soul that gets imprinted with all these impressions or karmic effects. Hinduism further elaborates that when a soul that gets polluted due to karmic effects, it needs to purify through repeated cycles of birth and death before it can merge with Brahman. One attains *Moksha* only when all the karmic effects are eliminated or extirpated. Those who believe in metempsychosis or reincarnation agree that the soul carries the impressions from one life to the next.

iii. The Three-Element Concept

We can also look at the soul and cosmic life energy as two different entities. Many philosophers profess that there is a soul in all living species, and a living body is a conjugation of soul and earthly ingredients. There is no disagreement with this postulate. But is life a conjugated outcome of body and soul only? Hypothetically, even when there will be no living species (and therefore no soul), the cosmic life energy will still remain with the potential to sprout and manifest universe and new lives. From this, we can postulate that life energy lies in a dormant form in the seeds, sperm, ova, etc., whereas the soul enters only when the potential life energy converts to kinetic life form. It follows, therefore, that cosmic life energy is different than the soul and has an independent identity apart from the soul. One day, someone raised a pertinent question. Where does this soul come from and where does it go at death if we subscribe to the postulate of three-element concept? The answer lies in the postulate that a soul cannot be conceptualised without a living species, and at the start of creation, there may not be any living species. Therefore, there may not have been any soul during such a period. But with the insertion of primordial life energy, living objects started forming and later, the cosmic energy itself may have constituted a primordial soul starting the cycle of transmigration with repeated births and deaths. If that is so, then a soul may appear from the vault of infinite cosmic energy and merge into the seminal seed at the end of an epoch.

It can thus be seen that three ingredients constitute a *jiva* (living species) and not two, which is the commonly held belief. The three ingredients are life energy, the soul, and the body. When these three conjoin together, a *jiva* is the resultant phenomenon. Such an approach might go against the accepted philosophy throughout centuries that there are only two elements in the constitution of life—*purusha* and *prakriti* (the spirit and body or the ethereal and the earthly), but to know the self, we will have to deliberate on the issue on a deeper level.

Two Element: Conceptual Difficulties

In the two-element concept, there are obvious conceptual difficulties. It is universally accepted that a body harbours a soul which can also be termed as the spirit, *atman*, or *ruh*. It is the energy element which inducts dynamism enabling living species to do all kinds of things. We have discussed that soul is an energy variant which arises from the cosmic energy. Though an energy variant, it carries impressions and gets polluted, which is an unfeasible idea so far as pure energy is concerned, as it always remains consistent. Therefore, life energy has to be different from the soul. This concept can be explained from the following examples.

Trees and plants transform the sun's energy to chlorophyll. You can add nutrients to plants so that they become healthier and more prone to garner more of the sun's energy. On the reverse, you can prevent nutrients to rob the ability of plants to convert the sun's energy to chlorophyll. In both these illustrations, we are not modifying the sun's energy but the instrument which exist due to the extension of energy. In a similar sense, you can use cardboard on a sunny day to obtain a shadow. You may change the shape of the cardboard and change the shape of the shadow but cannot alter the sun's energy. Basically, you cannot change sunlight to get a different shadow! Another example of this can be found in the various electric devices that we utilise. No matter how we may use our gadgets powered by electricity it does not affect the electric current; it remains as it was.

In a similar fashion, the soul is an abstruse extension of the cosmic energy. It is a modified template fashioned to gather impressions. Many philosophers equate the soul with the mind and perhaps, there is a valid justification for it. Both are abstract attributes resident with a living body. What we do in our life gets imprinted on the soul (or the mind), and when the soul transcends after the death of a being, it carries the gathered impressions or imprints. We must remember that anything we do in life creates an effect, and therefore, impressions are a natural corollary of living. The soul or the mind is an enabled extension of the cosmic energy to record imprints. At this juncture, it is important to recapitulate that the corporeal body is a conjugated outcome of cosmic and earthly energy, and therefore, it is natural that impressions are created to be recorded. The process is akin to lithography where imprints selectively aggregate on the lithograph plate. Generally, these imprints are called pollutants to the soul. But even when the soul becomes polluted, it is not necessary that the pure life energy is affected in any manner. Life energy remains as pure as it was while sprouting and sustaining a life. And if the purity of the life energy cannot be polluted then it has to be different than the soul. However, in the two-element concept, the life energy would lose its purity (if it is considered the same as the soul), since the soul would be the only cosmic element in a body, which certainly gets polluted and carries impressions life contributes. Thus, through the two-element concept, it is hard to explain how pure energy can get polluted or modified to carry life impressions.

There is another shortcoming of the two-element concept. We know that life energy resides in seeds in latent form. Given the right atmosphere, the seed would grow into a tall tree or plant one day. Similarly, life energy is dormant and latent in sperm and ova. Given the fusion and right support, it develops into a zygote and later into a child. However, the latent form of life energy in a seed, sperm, or ova does not possess a soul. When exactly does soul comes to reside in a forming body is not known but that a foetus embodies a soul is universally accepted. This process of the soul inhabiting a body is called ensoulment. During the time of Aristotle, it was widely believed that the soul enters the forming foetus at 40 to 90 days[12]

(40 days in case of a male embryo and 90 days in case of a female). St Augustine of Hippo (354-430 CE) speculated that abortion could only be a homicide once body formation occurred with ensoulment. Similarly, Thomas Aquinas (1224-1274 CE) believed that the foetus acquired human soul after 40 days of development[13] and therefore did not see abortion before ensoulment a harmful act. However, he condemned abortion at any stage of conception. Some other people thought that quickening (when the mother starts to feel the movements of the foetus) was an indication of ensoulment. Yet, the belief is that a growing human foetus embodies a soul only during later development. Fetal rights in Islam start from the moment of conception. The retribution is different before and after ensoulment. If the foetus is injured or aborted due to physical violence or attack by another person, the quantum of punishment (blood-money) is less than when the foetus is ensouled, and the 'life spirit' is breathed in, which, following the Islamic tradition, takes place after 120 days of conception.[14] By that time, the foetus is considered to be a fully-grown human being. In Hinduism, there is a wide variation in the belief of ensoulment. It varies from at the time of conception to the time the infant takes its first breath. There may be wide variance among philosophers and religions as to when ensoulment takes place in the womb, but still, one thing is clear that soul conjugation with a body takes place separately at a later stage of fetal development. Thus, one can surmise that life energy and soul are two different entities. Therefore, there are three entities to constitute a *jiva* or a living being, and not two.

That is as far as life energy and soul are concerned. But the bigger question is what is the priori force through which the material universe evolved, and the force with which the creation will fold into oblivion. If we consider cosmic energy as the force of creation, we must accept its presence in every speck of dust and every living species. Theistic God perceived in most religions remain sectarian and thus lack universalism in concept or application. Godly benevolence in sectarian religions remains limited to the sect of believers. And, therefore, logically, godly malevolence will also be limited to the clan of believers. It is apparent then that God, as perceived, cannot be the seminal force through which the whole material world came into existence and will fold when the time comes. That force has to be the cosmic energy which is self-born, omnipresent, omniscient, and omnipotent, permeating the whole of the universe. Also, equating God with nature would compromise the basic attributes of omnipotence and omniscience of God, as nature is an evolved phenomenon and not a priori, not a *Syambhu* (self-borne). Limiting God's visible concept to nature alone would compromise the third basic attribute of God—omnipresence. The presence of primaeval energy in every speck of the physical world and the universe, including in the living species, is a hard evidence that no one can refute. A parable in the Chandogya Upanishad appears relevant here:

"Uddalak proceeds to ask his son, Svetaketu, (who has returned from an ashram after 12 years of study) about the fundamental truth to which the son fumbles and finds himself unable to answer. Uddalak asks his son to put a piece of salt in a cup of water. The next day he asks him to produce the piece of salt, which was not possible as the salt had dissolved in water. The son dips his fingers in the cup and rummages through but cannot find it. Then Uddalak asks him to take a sip from the cup. Svetaketu first sips from the side and answers Uddalak, 'It is salty.' Uddalak then tells him to sip from the centre and asks how it is. Svetaketu again answers, 'Salty.' Then Uddalak sermonises his son about the nature of Brahman, 'Brahman pervades the whole universe. He is everywhere, in every speck of the universe, in you and me alike. And though we cannot see him, He is there. That is the true nature of Brahman, the Absolute Truth."

Cosmos is nothing but infinite cosmic consciousness, full of energy. Desire to manifest is the basic characteristic of the cosmos. Thus, the dream of cosmic consciousness is eternal as it manifests again and again. One of my Hindi poems (translated in English) tries to capture this theme:

"Let the earthly writings be wiped
From the slate of terrestrial expanse
Let the universe fold itself.
Dreams never die, they fold
Into seminal seed of creation
To sprout yet another manifestation!"

iv. Religion and Faith

Religion and faith are important factors in knowing the self as no discussion on mind, body, and soul can be complete without them.

Evolution of Religiosity

As stated earlier, a living species is a combination of earthy ingredients and life energy, also known as cosmic energy or universal consciousness. All ancient religions considered the cosmic force as the male element and the earth as the female part. In a similar context, Hindus considered divine energy as the male part and the earth as the female part. In the concept of *Ardhanarishwar*, Shiva has a male as well as a feminine side and is somewhat embodied presentation of the concept of anima and animus of Jungian philosophy. The religions of Egypt and Babylonia, like other ancient religions, were originally a fertility cult. The earth was female; the sun was the male.[15] Such a male-female concept has remained as the bedrock of religious philosophy in most ancient religions. This male-female concept appears extirpated in the Abrahamic faiths (Judo-Christian traditions), where God is conceptualised in the masculine gender; and finally, in Islam, where Allah is without an anthropomorphic representation or gender. But one thing is common in all these that there is an external force—a creationist God in Judo-Abrahamic religions, *purusha* and *prakriti* in the Hindu religion, cosmic energy or universal consciousness within 'Science of Reason' and atheistic sects—that unfolds as the manifested world.

Out of ignorance, man considers himself to be the creator and owner of worldly objects. At the beginning of human development, it is highly probable that man may have considered himself as the doer of everything. He engineered activities and exercised due control like hunting and gathering for food, building a shelter, managing rivers, creating aqueducts and canals, etc. But there were certain phenomenal changes that were not engineered by man. Death was one such phenomenon beyond human control. Many also believed in fate and destiny more than human capability. But due to not having any grasp or control over the life happenings, humanity developed the concept of an external agent that engineered such phenomena and thus developed the God-concept which, in turn, gave rise to a multitude of doctrines, hypotheses, and propositions.

Hereafter, man wondered about what happens after death. All religions believe in some version of afterlife. The ontological explanations may differ, but the crux is the same and a dominant factor for being religious is following the doctrines and rituals whereby a person feels to have indemnified and secured his afterlife.

To better understand 'why a religion' we need to look at man's fear of death. This insecurity is one of the vital reasons for the development of religious fervour. Man feels vulnerable when confronted with his insignificance and limitations, and thus searches for a tether to hold as a safeguard. And unable to find a tendril independent of time-space continuum in the material world, he veered towards an esoteric and ethereal power that could protect him and thus developed the god-concept. Whatever is obvious, one takes it for granted, but whatever is mysterious becomes symbolic. Religious development started with signs and symbols, culminating in icons and non-icons in multitude. To begin with, it could have been Animism that was for the whole living world. Should we not then say that Animism was closest to universal religion; religion for all? Humanity distanced from the universal faith as it climbed the ladder of progress, distanced from the kernel fact. This distance kept increasing, and now humanity stands at a crossroads from where ways separate out to different paths of ideas and abstracts, difficult to blend.

Religion is a thought, an idea asserted and followed by millions, whether it is factually valuable is difficult to say. Humanity has hardly gained anything from religion. In fact, religion has divided the human societies into groups and sects, and human history is remarkably inked with blood and tears shed in religious wars and conflicts! First, there were different religions and then religions within religion.

Scriptures dictate directly, or indirectly how should one behave, what should be its priorities, how should one interact in human society at large, what should be the basic beliefs, egalitarian tendencies, etc. But to prove their superiority, religious groups gradually developed fundamentalist and dogmatic attitudes and eventually became fountainhead of intolerance. One is asked to follow religious dictates and beliefs, generally without application of rationality. No doubt, there have been many enlightened souls explaining the gross and finer aspect of religion. But the number of such people is infinitely smaller compared to many who, claim to know their religious rituals, dogmatic beliefs, etc., but hardly know its essence.

Many Faiths in a Religion

Religion casts a deep impression on the individual's mind. The effects of religion and religious indoctrination are more relevant today than at any time in the past due to the multi-cultural, multi-ethnic, and multi-racial society we live in a shrunken world. Religion has two ingredients, the religiosity and the faith. It should not be viewed only through the lens of scriptures but also by the conduct of the followers as a religion is what one nurses within, whereas faith is what one practises. The religion of all Christians is the same, but the faith of Catholics and Protestants are different. And so, the faith of Unitarians that God is one person as opposed to the concept of 'the Father, Son, and Holy Spirit. A concept close to the *Advaita Vedanta.* For Unitarian Christians "Jesus was inspired by God in his moral teachings, but not a deity or God incarnate."[16]

Unitarianism is also known for the rejection of the doctrine of 'original sin' and predestination, that is the belief that events are willed by God with reference to the fate of an individual soul. Unitarians also place emphasis on the role of 'reason' in interpreting scriptures.[17]

In other words, it means that religion and scriptures can be rightly questioned and evaluated objectively. Take any religion, it consists of differing faiths. Sunni, Shia, Ahmadian, Bohra etc., are all followers of Islam but posit their faith in different concepts. Similarly, *Shaivites, Vaishnavites,* and *Shaktas* are all Hindus but nurse different faiths. Faith is more crucial in practical life than religion per se. The traditional Rabbinic Judaism believes that Moses received the Torah on Mount Sinai, whereas Samaritans (a sect of Judaism) revere Mount Gerizim and not Mount Sinai. Sadducees and Karaites believe only in the written Torah and not on the oral one. Various sects developed in Islam almost immediately after its founding. Such as the Shia sect which got further subdivided into many sub-sects. Similarly, many sub-sects, such as Hanafi, Maliki, Wahhabi, etc., developed in Sunni Islam. One can find similar examples in all the Indic religions as well, which include Nirguna, Vaishnavism, Shaivite, and Shaktism in Hinduism, Theravada, Mahayana, and Vajrayana in Buddhism, Digambar and Svetambara in Jainism, and Sanatana, Namdhari, and Nirankari in Sikhism.

Custodians of Faith

Faith gets twisted and modified by religious discourses and muddled interpretations of scriptures. Religious indoctrination also acts as a great influencer. It starts from one's childhood and carries on for the whole life and influences behaviour, biases, and tendencies. There are two important features in every religious order: one is, of course, the scriptural mandate, and the other is the group of people who claim ownership of religion or are designated as the 'custodians of faith'. They feed the general public their interpretation of the scriptures, and the people, short on time and patience, follow what is preached. This, more often than not, misguides the general public about the real purpose of religion and faith. Such religion heads have been termed as 'Hijackers of Faith' by the author Harb Pruthi in his book of the same title.[18] Pundits, mullahs, and evangelists take full advantage and pontificate on religious doctrines for their own personal motives. They generally claim to have a divine source and people believe them as the representatives of God. And these preachers can go to any extent to ensure that their words are accepted and carried far and wide. But the fact is that their teachings do not truthfully represent religious doctrines and the general public falls prey to them and easily catches onto these explanations and carry them in their minds. This primarily happens because most people do not have in depth knowledge of the scriptures and absorb whatever is explained to them by such 'custodians of faith'.

An important thing to realise here is that such religious teachers may not be erudite to know everything about the religion they preach and that they might not have all the answers to questions and doubts lurking in the mind of an individual. Externally, they might appear as genuine teachers till you delve deeper, their real sideshows. And when they fail to have an answer to a question, they just tell you to abide by what they preach as it has scriptural backing or hide behind religious sayings such as 'God is unknowable and undefinable' and 'God works in mysterious ways' etc. However, it is wrong to assume that scriptures cannot have a different interpretation other than theirs. So many sub-sects would not have developed in all the major religions unless it was interpreted differently, if not in letter but certainly in its spirit. All theological shifts have been based on differing interpretations of the scriptures. Each preacher likes you to believe that their interpretation is true, but there cannot be any 'true nature' of interpretations till the human mind thinks, confabulates, and remains sentient!

Interpreting Scriptures

Therefore, it is not correct to assume that rigid orthodoxy in religion has prevailed ever since its inception. It is, of course, evident that scriptural texts may not have undergone any change but the same is not true for its spirit. In other words, there may not have been any change in the texts, but changes have occurred in the spirit of religions due to different interpretations at different times. *Ramakrishna Paramhansa* (1836-1886), the Indian mystic maintained, "*jota mat tata path*" meaning thereby that there are as many ways as there are points of view. Newer sects continue to emerge even now because the human mind always conjures ideas and is never satisfied with one explanation. It is like trying to catch a shadow. Swami Vivekananda (1863-1902) says, "... so long as mankind thinks, there will be sects ... I pray that sects may multiply so that at last there will be as many sects as human beings, and each will have his own method, his individual method of thought in religion."[19] There may be a time in the future where every individual may have a personal religion of his own, and then religion will have no value in our life. The basic fact is that due to differing interpretations, newer ideas continue to emerge.

Successive religious heads and religious pundits have written volumes and volumes on the various interpretations of all the major religions. Sanatana Dharma discussed and wrote extensively to explain the divine in the form of Upanishads (there are 108 of them!). "The Upanishads give priority to revelations but never discourage intellectual inquiry."[20] One can find continuous debate, questions, and answers in Brihadaranyak Upanishad on spiritual topics such as body, soul, divinity, Brahman, life, and death. Theological discussion and religious explanation are parts of religious practice of a sentient mind. A Sentient mind is basically a questioning mind. One finds extensive theological discussion in all the religions of the world, not only in Hinduism, and expect differences being resolved by frank discussion but nothing of that sort ever happens. Religious pundits always try to prove the superiority of their religion by denigrating other religions. At one side this appears right to enter into frank discussions, but the flip side is that the freedom to interpret also allows religious teachers an advantage to catch people in a wrongful bind from where it becomes difficult to extricate. That, primarily is the fault line preventing social integration between different religious communities and ethnic groups. Man continues to search for a universal religion, religion for all. Question is can that be possible? The simple answer, of course, is 'not likely' due to the ego of religious superiority.

Superiority in Religion

It is well-known that every religion harps upon their superiority and preaches supremacy of their tenets and philosophy. Proponents of any religion make it appear that a particular doctrine is the last word of the Almighty, which cannot be challenged, changed, or altered. Any doubt raised on theistic belief was considered a heretic. Till the 17th century or so, any new idea which was not in conformity with the Bible was considered a sacrilege. So basically, all proselytising theistic religions started dividing mankind into two groups of people: those who are on the 'correct path' and those who are not. The theology of correct and incorrect path started with the development of monotheism, such as Judaism. Old Testament divides humanity into two categories of chosen people and the gentiles. Islam divides human society into believers and non-believers. In its basic concept, Hinduism considers the whole world as one family—*Vsudhaiva Kutumbakam*. "The Vedic tradition welcomes any religion or faith . . . Unapparelled are the Vedic ideals that declare "A religion is not a religion at all if it asserts its superiority over other faiths."[21]

Personal beliefs may contrast with larger social beliefs. Extrapolating this argument, religious doctrines can be said to be not in sync with the holistic concept of wellness of humanity and therefore, not universal. When evangelists preach that all heathens will burn in eternal hellfire, followers of that religion start strongly believing in such a precept. And in the process, they develop a sort of fundamentalist behaviour and outlook, clinging closely to their religious teachings, and denigrating others. This, in turn, leads to a negative attitude towards other religious groups. But the question is whether precepts such as 'all heathens will burn in eternal fire in hell' is true or not. No one knows as there is simply no way to know the truth. It is all guesswork but believers hold it to be true. Such precepts are used to instil fear in the minds of people as well as to provide an argumentative handle in the hands of evangelists.

Personal beliefs transform into a collective belief resulting in ideological and religious conflicts. Religious conflicts will continue to divide human society unless humanity lets go the ego of religious superiority. No logic can justify ill-treating and tormenting people of another religious community just because they do not follow your religious doctrine. The problem is not religious diversity but dogmatic and rigid beliefs. The fact is that a faith which shows intolerance towards other faiths cannot be universal. More importantly, all, even atheists, have a fundamental right to exist. Atheism is also an idea, a sect, just like a religion. Therefore, such a negative belief about heathens, *kaffirs*, and gentiles is illogical. If there is an Almighty, He is universal and transcendental. He is the source of everything in the universe; all are His painting, His work, His creation, and all are His children. The Creator cannot be parochial or sectarian to his creation and hold that this is right and that is wrong. Therefore, presumptive dictates in such a faith will not be in line with the divine dictates of the Almighty. David Frawley (Pandit Vamadeva Shastri), an American Hindu theologian, points out, "The exclusivist idea of religion may have one God but it has two humanities—the believers and the non-believers and regards the non-believers as inferior or sinful who are either to be converted or conquered, which leads to every sort of misunderstanding and exploitation."[22] Religion, after all, is nothing but a collective concept of an esoteric power that created and sustains the universe, flora and fauna, and humanity on the earth. Even if we consider the existence of a creationist God, His munificence has to be necessarily embedded in all. Only then its relevance can be validated.

Sectarian and Universal Approach

The philosophical approach to any religion should be in its universal application. Whether it is followed practically or not is another matter. Mankind has walked a long distance on the road to find a universal religious order, discovered and rediscovered newer ideas, and doctrines, but the journey remains short of the destination. As stated earlier, the most ancient way of worshipping may have contained only a symbolic representation of the supernatural power. But slowly and gradually mankind realised the importance of both, the heavenly and terrestrial, and started respecting not only the supernatural but also the terrestrial. To represent this concept, philosophers coined the term 'Animism'. Animism considers that all terrestrial objects, be it living or inanimate possess a spiritual essence. Ontologically, one may find Animism as the most ancient way of worship. Some may group it in religion, but it was perhaps a way of life, and not a religion., certainly not an organised religion. Over succeeding periods, Animism gave way to polytheism, where iconic gods were crafted and named differently for different aspects pertaining to human life. It is remarkable to note that the polytheists developed god figures and deities for each human attribute, energy, well-being, health, knowledge, wealth, spiritual and physical strength, etc. From polytheism developed monotheistic religions, as somewhere mankind conceptualised that it was not necessary to accept many gods with partial powers but have an all-powerful single abstract figure. It is not wrong to assume that at some point in time, people got fed up with polytheistic concept and found a simple formula, the concept of a unique all-powerful god, instead of different gods with partial powers. All powers enjoined by different deities were thus bundled in one abstraction. With this, attributes such as anger and benevolence as well as malevolence and contemptuousness also got carried into the nature of the 'one-God' concept in monotheism. However, there was an apparent contradiction. Monotheists conceived the all-powerful God to be omniscient and pure without any negative attributes. But religious pundits realised that human life was full of not only joy but also grief and misery. To explain this, all joyful tidings in life were attributed to the pristine, singular God and all evil to another independent but parallelly developed concept of the 'anti-god'. This polar opposite of God was termed as *Ahriman (Angra Mainyu)* in the Zoroastrian religion, Satan in Christianity, and *Shaitan* or *Iblis* in Islam.

Shifts in Religious Beliefs

Such shifts were not without other problems. It created doubts and the clash of ideas. Stephen Greenblatt sums it up in his book, *The Rise and Fall of Adam and Eve*, "This reduction to one supreme divinity. . . [and] doing away with multiple gods introduces certain problems . . . Did the wise maker not anticipate what his creatures would do?"[23]

In that case, perhaps He lacked clairvoyance, which cannot be true for an omniscient and omnipotent God. The question that whether religiosity has been good for mankind or not is not relevant as millions follow one or another religion. The important question is whether the past was wholly extirpated while humanity embarked on the path of a new religion, newer way of worship, and newer philosophy about the esoteric? And the answer is 'no' as religious progress has had a periodic development and has carried some elements from the past. The fact remains that while stepping from animism to polytheism and from polytheism to monotheism, mankind carried something from the discarded past beliefs. Polytheistic Hindu religion carried the universal approach of Animism. Catholic Christianity (Protestants do not subscribe to such a concept considering it subscribing to idolatry) in its flowering created the concept of patron Saints (clearly drawing from polytheism) to protect and help overcome difficulties. Some examples of this include England was protected by St George, Scotland by St Andrews, Hungary by St Stephen, and France by St Martin.[24] They also adopted god-figures for cities, such as St Ambrose for the city of Milan and St Mark for Venice. Not only that, but there were patron saints for professions and sickness, too, just like the polytheistic concept, something like the ancient Greeks, and instant Hindus. Islam took many aspects from Judaism and Christianity. Mythical stories were carried from the Old Testament and incorporated in Islamic theology. The practice of circumcision was taken, most likely from Judaism and the concept of *shaitan* was adopted from Christianity (Circumcision was practised in many ancient societies). But Judo-Abrahamic religions adopted it in the belief that many of their prophets, Moses downwards were born without a foreskin—an example of how a mythical belief can turn to a rigid religious practice. Buddhism and Jainism, too, carried many ideas, parables, and mythical stories from Hinduism. The purport is that past cultural and doctrinal influences were not wholly severed and few things from previous beliefs and religious practices were carried in the building blocks of newer religions. History of religious development has been linear with comma and semicolon, but never reached a full stop. In fact, it may not reach a full stop so long as man thinks!

A shift in terms of the attributes of God happened with the transition from Judaism to Christianity. It is important to remember that Jesus of Nazareth was born a Jew. Realising that God cannot be malevolent, he proposed a different concept that God cannot be angry and punishing as a father cannot be contemptuous to his progenies and advocated that God was all loving and merciful. The fear-element and malevolence in Judaism to discipline humanity changed to universal love in Christianity. Thus, we find two important shifts in religious history. One was the transition to a single all-powerful God concept, and second, was whitewashing the figurative representation of a god. Islam borrowed many ideas and practices from Judaism and Christianity (the earlier Abrahamic religions), just like Christianity borrowed from Judaism. But it developed as an independent religion with well-defined social norms, universal brotherhood (for the Muslim Community), and legal provisions with a strict set of punishments and retributions. Thus, a firm and direct bond was created between man and the Almighty with an element of fear as well as of munificence with clearly defined aims and objectives. With all such developments, the concept of polytheism was discarded in favour of a single all-powerful God in monotheism.

Is Religion a Heresy?

Let us once again recall that initially there may have been only one religion or one way to worship. Different religions developed later as the human colonies diversified. Point to note here is that each religion considered the past as well as the later religions inferior, and possibly heretical. Therefore, any religion as developed and practiced by man is a heretic! Does it sound contradictory? One can turn around and say how can a religion be a heretic! Acts and ideas can be a heretic, a person can be a heretic, but how can a religion be a heretic? According to Adi Shankara (788-820 CE), the Indian philosopher and theologian, "A seeker of Truth is the thinker who brings a mind free from preoccupation, a mind cleansed of all impurities by discipline and culture . . . to receive and understand the highest truth . . . He repeatedly urges the need to bring an open mind to the study of philosophy."[25] Just close your eyes, wipe out all religious indoctrination from your mind, and then think about it, objectively.

Consider there is no religion, only humanity. Consider sapiens have just entered the stage of the created universe. Collectively they weave an idea . . . idea of collective identity, mutual respect, and concern towards nature and the universe. Let us call it 'omnibus religion', a religion of mutual respect, acceptance, and tolerance; a collective idea which does not discriminate based on different concepts, different groups, and different clans. And then religion subsequently developed and practiced their faith which did not appear to be universally conscious of the whole humanity. Now look at it differently. Monotheistic religions would consider polytheistic way with idolatry heretical as monotheism professes a single all-powerful god. And Christianity, where God is depicted to have a son (Christ) who is human as well as divine. The omnibus religion at the most ancient human settlement would, therefore, consider all such religious diversities heretical as it differed from the fundamental religious concept and did not stand for the whole of humanity and nature. At the same time, any new religious concept that developed would consider the previous religious doctrine heretical. So, it is both the ways. Older religions would consider newer religions heretical, and vice-versa. Once we say a section of the human being is expendable and that whatever is in nature is to be exploited for the pleasure of man, we fall in the trap of being a heretic in the eyes of the religion of humanity-primordial omnibus religion. The human being is far removed from achieving a commonality in religious thoughts, concept, and practice, and the distance is increasing by the day.

Omnibus Religion for All

The only way humanity can achieve commonality is to accept and tolerate all thoughts, all concepts, and all religions. There is no need to vilify the earlier held belief, to prove superiority, but just to accept and tolerate all different religions and faiths and become a follower of the common omnibus religion. There is no conversion, no baptism!

However, we know that it may never happen as mankind has drunk the hemlock of religious ego! The idea of religion at best is a subjective outcome of human thoughts. We accept a God-concept as we conjure. Not only different communities but even two different individuals may have differing views of the Supernatural Being. The totality of how you perceive God may be quite different than your close friend, or even your spouse, though you may belong to the same religious group. The subject-object relationship is highly individualistic and subjective, as the individual mind is involved. Let us look at it from a different angle. We all think that what we see around is what it is, but each individual will have a different worldview. My worldview and yours will be different and we two may spend years debating but never reach a consensus. Mind you, the object has remained the same for you and me, but interpretations are different. All perceptions, sensation, and observation have a subjective personal append. Erwin Schrodinger, the Nobel winning physicist, while tracing the history in the issue of subject-object relationship, in his highly acclaimed book, *What Is Life?*, says, "There were few, if any, who did not emphasise that all our sensations, perceptions, and observations have a strong, personal subjective tinge and do not convey the nature of the thing-in-itself, to use Kant's term."[26]

* * *

Since the beginning, humanity has tried to find a commonality in religion, including disbelief in the theistic concept, but failed. There are many prominent thinkers and philosophers as well as a considerable section of the general public that does not believe in the god-concept. Many sects, such as *Charavakas,* atheists, and hedonists, do not abide by the idea of a god. In a somewhat similar mode, Buddhism and Jainism also do not believe in any creationist or unique God but posit their concept on cause and effect. The Buddha (480-400 BCE) suggested that it was fear that produced religious impulse in humanity.[27]

The essence of any religion should be to spread love and respect for all, the whole humanity, accept all different thoughts and ideas, and nurture the good part. But how many can we find in the world who believe in such altruistic principles? The general public remains rivetted around religious ideas as preached, and live a religious life like gin horses moored to a pole. The mind is not allowed to deliberate. Most religions (at least theoretically) espouse well for humanity and tend to uplift mankind to an upper spiritual platform but hold that it may be only through their way.

Moreover, just to appear good, we generally say that all religious doctrines are universally good; bid well for the whole humanity, whereas the ground reality could be quite different. Religiosity bases on three legs-the embedded philosophy, the scriptures, and its practice. While the philosophy of all religions may be the same, that is to take mankind to higher plane towards emancipation, the scriptures deviate from this basic theme, and the practice; deviate vastly. Monotheism professed that their unique god was the only concept that may be worshipped, others being false gods. In the understanding that others are 'false gods', one conceptually acknowledged the presence of other gods (which in itself is a wrong concept as god cannot be two or three). That apart, singularity in any religion leads to the singularity of mind. It restricts thoughts and lays fetters on the free-thinking. On a deeper and dispassionate analysis, one is likely to conclude that a polytheist is less likely to develop religious fundamentalism.

What is written in the scriptures may be good as scriptures are full of sermons on human value, societal brotherhood, and universal and natural laws. But the mind gets conditioned to one way of thinking and refractive to other ideas. Religious faith and dogmatic beliefs create a mental block by encapsulating the human mind, whereas progressive life demands change. And unless there is the freedom to think change and progress cannot be made. I find no better example than to narrate what happened in the Christian world. As late as till the 17th century, the Christian Church held that sun rotated around earth. When scientists discovered that it was the other way around, they were declared a heretic and punished.

Inquisitors burnt Bruno at stake; Galileo was imprisoned and tormented. This happened only due to embedded belief in a theology casting strong fetters over the mind. One was expected not to think beyond theological belief and discard the regularly appearing evidence to the contrary in the scientifically advancing world. Discoveries are not only based on intuitive sparks but also on observation, analysis, and contemplation. Scientific advancement takes place on rationality and intuition. The spark generates in the mind, and then comes the logic, parameters, and proof. Some may call it creativity—the essence of social advancement. When the heliocentric concept was accepted, mental binds got loosened, and the Christian world accelerated on the road of scientific discoveries enriching human life!

God did not create a religion; it is we, the humans who conjured the idea of religion with scriptures, and with innumerable sets of practice and rituals. Baruch Spinoza talking about God, says, "The multitude ever prone to superstition, and caring more for the shreds of antiquity than for eternal truth, pays homage to the books of Bible, rather than to the word of God"[28]; clearly hinting that mankind laid greater belief on the scriptures than God. One is so tightly bound with rituals and anthropomorphic images, idols, iconic or non-iconic ideas, and scriptures that one views these as the Absolute Truth. Any wrong turn, a wrong way, or incorrect posture during a ritual worship sets in an alarm bell, a sense of scare. The pith of any religion lies in your heart as faith, not in the idols and rituals. One should worship through the idols, rituals, and scriptures, not the idols, rituals, and scriptures. Swami Vivekananda taught, "An idol serves the same purpose for a religious devotee as a flag does for an army."[29] The problem is that the human mind is conditioned. It always looks for name and form (*nama* and *rupa*) and tries to deify the divine with a name and a form. Man has tried unsuccessfully to find utopia through religious diversity or through brilliant ideas. And in the process has created huge dams in the social order.

Temporal Social Order and Religion

Many also consider concepts such as fascism, Marxism, capitalism, and communism as religions. One may say that these sectarian ideas are products of human endeavour to find the best possible social order but how can these be considered as a religion? The thing to note here is that religion is also an idea created by man and tends to construct a social order with a unique cultural and collective propensity. Nonetheless, religious concepts in whatever form impacted political arrangements over centuries and still cast a strong influence on political systems of many countries. Bertrand Russell (1872-1970) writes in his book, *A History of Western Philosophy*, "Temporal powers in some way dominated over man's thoughts and feelings . . . progressively destroyed what remained of the Roman belief in unity of civilisation."[30]

Communism and Fascism are examples of how a temporal power could dominate the minds of its citizen. Sadly, in its wake million lives were lost, and millions uprooted. That is the price humanity has paid to an idea. Similarly, humanity has paid a heavy price on changing religious beliefs and tectonic theological shifts causing havoc and large-scale destruction, much worse than natural disasters in the term of lives lost. History is replete with examples where religion and state were so intricately connected that nothing was permitted unless it had a religious sanctity. The pope anointed emperors and expected them to safeguard Catholic interest the world over. Religious adversity resulted in conflicts within and outside the empire. About two centuries of crusades between Catholic Christians and Islam is a perfect example of such religious strife. Dostoevsky, through the character Ivan Karamazov in the novel *The Brothers Karamazov*, puts it succinctly, "For the sake of common worship they have slain each other with the sword. They set up gods and challenged one-another. 'Put away your gods and come and worship ours, or we will kill you and your gods!'"[31]

Take any religion and you will find that the basis of religious conflicts has been the preaching that only 'their way' assures salvation. Swami Vivekananda says, "We find that nothing that has brought man more blessings than religion, yet there is nothing that has brought him more horror than religion. Nothing has made the brotherhood of man more tangible than religion; nothing has bred more bitter enmity between man and man than religion."[32]

Thus, we see that both religion and sectarian ideas are constructs of the human mind. The only difference being that the end-effect of religion remains wrapped in a mist, whereas the outcome of sectarian ideologies (communism, fascism, etc.) can be seen and felt in the temporal world; and reviewed.

Value of Religion . . . If at All

If one thinks purely with his rational mind without any preconceived notions, one might reach a conclusion that 'religion is an unintelligent expression of human wisdom'. Even though the religious fervour has been heavily berated by some of the most eminent philosophers and thinkers, the fact remains that religion is the earliest and most fundamental idea that developed on which human mind remains riveted. So, is religion all bad? When this question arises, I am forced to concede that religion may have some value after all. It tends to discipline the ever-wandering human mind from sinful thoughts and acts. It might not be possible to quantify how useful religion has been, but fundamentally, it tends to restrict baneful ideas leading to anti-social and destructive activities. There is also another angle to it—religion can act as a balm to human suffering. It is usual that if some overawing and debilitating grief befalls on an individual and the person feel helpless, he turns to the divine. Thus, he gets some relief from mental suffering and turmoil. One may recapitulate the famous dictum of Karl Marx that 'religion is the opium of the people'.[33] Many have questioned this quote appearing independent of the statement preceding it which is hardly quoted: The full quotation is "Religion is the sigh of oppressed culture, heart of heartless world, and soul of soulless conditions, religion is the opium of the people." It is, therefore, evident that his remarks were different than what is typically believed. It offers succour to the suffering of humanity.

Humanity continues to make efforts to find the shape of a final religion which applies to all, accepted by all, and relevant to the whole humanity, whole creation without discrimination. But such an effort is not likely to meet success mainly due to man's ego. Religion is basically a sectarian belief and each sect, or the religious community thinks his way to be the best. Another factor is that in the case of religious development, the final stage of evolution can never be reached, and therefore there could be nothing final in this regard. Religious, cultural, and mental growth is a continuous process and is subject to change with time. Unfortunately, some consider a discussion on religious doctrines heretic.

Each religion will necessarily have the worldview following their own belief, including religious dogma. And when one considers his faith as undisputable, he fails to consider the welfare of humanity as a whole. Moreover, human beings are not the sole expression of creation; there are many others (animate and inanimate) that reside in this vast existence and all need to be respected. We worship the Almighty in one form or the other because it is the source of life force. But just creating life isn't enough; it has to be sustained as well. The environment supports life and therefore, must be respected. Rivers, oceans, and other water bodies support terrestrial life. Similarly, plants, trees, and forests all support life and are objects of reverence. Hindus worship trees, forests, rivers, and oceans to show respect in the same way they worship the divine. So even though the divine is revered as the provider of life, nature needs to be respected and worshipped for its contribution towards sustaining life. But man, with his rigid religious beliefs and sense of superiority considers all in nature to be exploited. The present scenario can change only when humanity realises the folly of dogmatic and rigid belief and moves towards the domain of spirituality.

v. Spirituality

Retaining a holistic concern for the whole of humanity and the creation in the heart, is in essence, spirituality. It should any day be more important than nurturing only the religious fervour. And though the formative grounds for spirituality maybe religion and faith, its dimension is much broader than the communal aspect of any religion. Spirituality follows a stepladder pattern to meet the ever-growing spiritual need of mankind. So, when one follows only a religious path, he gets blinded by the rigid dogmatic beliefs that form the framework of a religion. Going a step further, we very well assume that spirituality without a God-figure is the right path. Spirituality provides liberation from tightly held religious bindings. Against this, some may argue that religion, supposedly being the bedrock of spirituality, cannot be completely divested. Such contrariety will exist unless mankind moves away from dogmatic beliefs. Spirituality is often confused with religion but it is different. We will discuss how and why in succeeding paragraphs.

Why Spirituality?

For thousands of years, humanity has believed in the existence of supernatural power which can mend or destroy the worldly life. The concept of religion remains at the centre of the individual psyche and collectively, in society and community. Almost from the beginning of the time, people have believed in God and spirit simply because others in their social circle and ethnic community do so. The Hindus, the Muslims, and the Christians, or for that matter, followers of any religion accept religious doctrines since they believe these to have come from a supernatural power. They take the teachings and beliefs as infallible. But due to the factors explained in earlier chapters, people started questioning the validity of God-concept.

The lure of a greater objective to a reach higher platform was required to bind the human mind into virtuous thinking and doing good for himself as well as nature and humanity. That object could be a religious ladder reaching out to a platform of emancipation and salvation. Therefore, religion developed as the most important factor to shape and regulate individual behaviour. How much it succeeded, if at all, is a matter of discussion. They looked for another way to realise the divine and thus developed the concept of spirituality.

* * *

At first glance, spirituality appears akin to religiosity, but on deeper reflection, it is different as it rejects religious dogma and divisive ethos of a religion. If the man-made idea of religion encouraged dogmatism and sectarianism, then such ideas were rejected in the pursuit of spirituality. Religious belief is an assumption, a preconceived notion and it does not define the divine, common to all. If any religion would have, so many religions may not have developed. The basic concept in theology, more so in the monotheistic faiths, is encapsulating, whereas spirituality tends to be unbinding and goes beyond religious fetters. Religion occupies much vast area on the mental plate. Spirituality, on the other hand, occupies little space in our mental frame. That is because religion, through revelations, myths, and parables, appears tangible, whereas spirituality remains a distant domain enwrapped in even deeper abstraction. The mind has to decondition in order to free it from ritualistic and dogmatic religious teachings and beliefs. The bird of free-thinking gets entrapped in the religious cage. Whereas spirituality is the vast sky where clouds must float unhindered. Looking back at the past history of religious conflicts one is bound to conclude that religion by itself has failed to achieve the desired objectives of virtuous thinking, pious living, and emancipation. Thus, the need for spirituality.

Aims and Objectives of Spirituality

Let's have a closer look at what spirituality entails. Pursuance of happiness is one of the fundamental aims in life. Man, through religion and science has tried to know 'life' itself but failed. When we try to unravel the mystery of life, we encounter a virtual wall beyond which we know lies the secret of life, but we are unable to see. That is where rationality fails and spirituality becomes relevant. Spirituality is a bridge or a virtual line on a drawing board trying to connect implicit dots through religion, as it tends to pertain to the whole of humanity. Scriptures dictate what should be one's behaviour and how one should live, and on the face value, it appears egalitarian. However, how far these have been followed remains a matter of conjecture. Doctrines bind the mind, not allowing it to think otherwise and thus circumscribe people to a set of doctrines—religious and worldly. And in all such cases, ethical mandates and dictates are hardly followed. From the edicts of Hammurabi (C-1772 BCE) to present, one finds that religions have laid commandments as to how one should think and behave but how many believe and practice in the edict of 'love thy neighbour', or 'do unto others as you would do to yourself'? If all the religious commandments and dictates were followed by all, we may have been living in a utopian world, devoid of envy, greed, anger, and bitterness. But we know nothing of that sort has happened. We know that to do away with envy and greed is not that simple, primarily due to ego, but also due to living in a society divided by religion where sectarianism prevails.

Religion makes a person refractive to other ideas. The basic approach in the quest of spirituality is to be egalitarian and be concerned for the welfare and upliftment of the whole humanity. In other words, one needs to discard sectarianism, the fundamental attribute in any religion, and practice humanism. In the search of spirituality, the mind must transcend religious binds and only then one may aspire to climb the spiritual ladder. It may not be possible to discard religion and uproot religious practices but it is always possible to look for and identify a religious order, or the egalitarian part in a religion close to humanity.

Spirituality beyond Religiosity

Reminiscing about my childhood days, I can visualise my mother sitting at the fore of the worship room (*pooja ghar*) reading through Ramayana, Sukhsagar, or any other Hindu scriptures. I can visualise my father working out issues concerning tax collection, remittances, etc., of his zamindari. Many times, he remitted a substantial percentage or even the total agrarian tax in case of drought and flooding. If there was a problem in the village, they were empathetic and tried to help as much as possible. My father was held in extremely high esteem in society. One incidence I vividly recall. After the abolition of zamindari system, he was busy winding up the state. He sold a large piece of land at a distant village, which he thought could be difficult to manage in the absence of the zamindari machinery. One evening, some buyers had come to deposit the money. Our munshi was entering the records in his diary when my father remarked nonchalantly, "Hey folks, you all are not taking any receipt, and supposing I deny tomorrow having received the money for the sale of land, what will happen then?" In the same calm manner, the primary buyer remarked, "What will happen? We will think that the sun has risen from the West, instead from the East!" That was the standing my father enjoyed in the area. It was the spiritual standing beyond the temporal powers that he enjoyed as a zamindar of the area.

My mother worshipped almost everything under the sun and kept fasts frequently following the religious calendar. She observed practically all Hindu festivals, prayed not only through the idols and symbols, but also trees, water wells, the sun, and the moon with equal devotion and fervour. She also believed in human values more than fasting and festivals. One can say that she was more spiritually inclined than religious. There are many anecdotes but to acquaint the readers with her spiritual mindset, I will quote one. During my transit from one place to another during the 1965 Indo-Pak war, I stopped at Patna for a day. My parents had come from the village to meet. In a family gathering, my mother remarked, "I had counselled you not to join the armed forces, but you did not listen." She thought I was going to the front line, whereas the fact was that a doctor in the Air Force was rarely required to confront the enemy face to face, as an infantry soldier. Whatever may have been her limited knowledge or ignorance about the army and war, she, after a while, commented as if speaking to herself, "But those who fight the war at the front are also sons of some mother." clearly a spiritual reflection. My parents led a very peaceful life as they passionately believed that peace is a state of mind, not obtainable through money, bargain or barter, or even with religious rituals and practices. They were religious but much more spiritual. Both my parents believed in humanity more than religion. And they rode the rough and smooth alike, with equanimity.

Spirituality: Past and Present

For a long time in the past, the Western philosophers indeed equated spirituality as being synonymous with religion. But during the latter part of the 19th century, this understanding started to change and philosophers, as well as theologians, started to see the difference. In 1866, English critic, Walter Peter, wrote that the spiritual side of life was 'simply the passion for inward perfection', which had no necessary connection with religion. There, of course, was a hue and cry, and a detractor howled that Peter was trying to 'promote spirituality without God.'[34]

But now it is universally accepted that spirituality is somewhat different than religion. It is different but not totally detached.

In the current age, people see spirituality as much more relevant to humanity than any organised religion. According to a study conducted by 'Pew Research Center' in 2012, the number of Americans who did not identify with any religion increased from 15 per cent in 2007 to 20 per cent in 2012, and this number continues to grow. Of these religiously unaffiliated Americans, 37 per cent classified themselves as spiritual but not religious, while 68 per cent said they did not believe in God, and 58 per cent felt a deep connection to the Earth.[35]

Such a tectonic shift in religious affiliation is not new. Formation of Theosophical Society in 1875 CE by Helena Blavatsky was an effort to dissociate from organised religion. This sentiment has become more prevalent than ever as more and more people are seeing religion as a dividing than a unifying force. In this context, it is important to understand that any religious base must espouse the well-being of all, transcending denominational and religious barriers. Only then religion will become pragmatic and synonymous with spirituality. A point of concern some people raise is that turning to spirituality could diminish religious fervour, but nothing of that sort is ever going to happen. The fact remains that "Neither morality nor religion can be said to be in danger so long as man is conscious of his finitude."[36]

Religion and spirituality are not contradictory but complementary with some conditions. It is important to realise that religious affiliation, howsoever strong, can never perfectly blend with spirituality unless one is prepared to rise above sectarianism and transcend the narrow religious dogma and belief.

Spirituality and Dharma

As discussed, spirituality means illumining the inner sense of a being by realising the universal sense of interrelatedness and living under the radiance of divinity. For a deeper understanding of spirituality, one must realise the *Dharma* of humanity. The concept of *Dharma* is central to Indian philosophy. It is not bound by religion and includes statute law, practice, custom, individual character, innate tendencies, etc.—all the qualities and aspects that make a human being humane. *Dharma* is a Sanskrit word for which an exact translation in Western languages is difficult to find. The closest term is 'religion', but *Dharma* encompasses religion, culture, expected duties and responsibilities, and egalitarian tendencies in a person, not only religion. In simple terms, it means what one bears— the envelop within which a personality remains encased with tendencies and predilection. For example, the innate tendency of water is to flow to a lower gradient and cool anything that comes in contact, so that is its *Dharma*. Similarly, it is the innate quality of fire to burn, so that would be its *Dharma*. It is the *Dharma* of a government or a king is to govern well. It is the *Dharma* of a warrior to protect the citizen. In the present-day context, it is the *Dharma* of news reporters to report truthfully. Whether one abides by these or not is another matter. Aspiring for salvation, essentially through egalitarian tendencies, would be the *Dharma* of human beings. The antonym of *Dharma* is '*Adharma*', that is anything—a thought, an action, a tendency, or predilection—against the principles of *Dharma*. It is the bounden duty of every individual to try to follow the path of *Dharma*, that is being humane. Spirituality is the way forward for attaining such a state.

Spirituality (Detachment) and Ego (Attachment)

When a person embarks on the spiritual path, he looks at love, envy, greed, hatred, etc., with equanimity. He does not care for material wealth but only for altruistic refinements. This set of people renounce the world to realise the divine. They do that to remain away from worldly attachments, which may distract them from pursuing the path to salvation. For an ascetic, ridding attachment takes place in stages. Getting away from the mundane world is the first stage. Saints and ascetics go to higher reaches of Himalayas to engage in penance, and many spend years in one of the innumerable caves that dot the Himalayas just by themselves with minimum life support. It provides him freedom from mundane activities and frees his mind to concentrate on the divine. That is one way in the effort towards salvation. Nevertheless, it may not be necessary to climb the Himalayas for penance to practise spirituality.

A saint goes to the Himalayas to detach himself but a householder practices unattachment from his surroundings as he cannot get away from the usual mundane objects. Mind you there is a difference between these two terms. When you say 'I am detached' the connotation is that you have already separated the object, whereas when you say 'I am unattached' it means that object is still around but you have no attraction to it. Therefore, an unattached householder is at a greater height of penance than an ascetic.

In both these cases (attachment and detachment), one needs to introspect and have a strong resolve. One detaches himself from others in the immediate surroundings, then the society, then his belongings, including wealth, and finally, the self. Detachment does not mean giving away all your possession, rather it is a sense where you have no undue love to mundane worldly possessions. This is easily said than done. Only when one detaches himself from his ego, he will be able to detach from self. Detachment from self is the most important but most difficult part of the whole exercise as ego prevents one from suppressing the ego-ness, since self is the *raison d'etre* of one's existence in the material world. A sage, seer, or hermit may conquer sinful human attributes with detached living but not the ego of being. The ego of being is fundamental to self-identity. It is through the ego of being one realises he exists. The purport is, even if one preaches to discard all types of human attributes, the one which remains is the ego of being. Man feels important being a part of cosmos.

Once a person jettisons his ego, he realises himself to be a part of the whole of humanity. He will find greater joy and happiness in sharing the grief and suffering of others. An egalitarian outlook purifies the mind and heart. As a result, it springs a stream of compassion that wipes remnant traces of selfishness. Such a person will naturally obtain freedom from the whirlwind of ego, desire, and attachment. Anyone who embarks on the path of spirituality is more likely to experience the divine, compared to a person whose mind remains fettered within the confines of a religion. In essence, the foremost requirement for spirituality is giving away the sense of ego and the sense of 'I'-ness.

However, when a person embarks on the path of detachment, he may find it difficult to detach completely from the material world. Still, with an open mind, intellect, and rational introspection, one may be able to break many self-created girdled chains in which he is bound. The mind, in that case, obtains a stage of tranquillity known as *Sthitiprajya.* It is a Sanskrit word meaning a detached, balanced, and dispassionate outlook. Sense of grief for a person who maintains a *Sthitiprajya* mental state will be much less pronounced and cause a minimal negative effect. This is because how a person takes an episode of grief is determined by the state of his mental balance. The Buddha resolved this by saying, *"Janmah dukhah."* It means that life is full of grief and it cannot be wished away. But its impact can be mitigated or overcome if you consider the incident causing grief as a 'thing'. There are many things you come across in day-to-day life and each may cause grief or happiness, satisfaction, or disappointment. Thus, a person whose mind is immersed in the self will feel the deleterious impact of grief much more than a person who is *Sthitiprajya* and spiritually inclined.

Unfortunately, most of us possess a self-centric mind buffeted by egotistic behaviour. The ego leads to greed. Those who have amassed wealth and power are in even a tighter grip of ego. One may wonder what is wrong in amassing wealth even with dubious means as it affords a comfortable life. But one must understand that dubious means will create negative vibes in the mind of the individual and perpetuate either physical or mental harm. Such people always live in the fear of being discovered and therefore try to cover their tracks. In the process, they indulge in more and more sinful acts, creating more and more negative vibes. If someone commits a deceitful act or cheats another person, he will develop negative vibrations in his mind which will keep tormenting him. Within the framework of deceit, many other traits develop, which in due course, occupy a core niche and cast a perpetual shadow on all the squares of the chessboard of one's personality. The concept of competitiveness comes from our animal instinct. Predators are known to chart out their area of influence. Human beings also try and define their area of influence, be it physical or ideological. The human nature is such that envy, deceit, capricious behaviour, etc., are inbuilt features. If not properly dealt with and controlled, it can cause immense mental and bodily harm. It is explained as follows:

> In this discussion, one must subsume that thought is an energy variant. Any energy will affect cells in the body. To kill cancer cells, doctors subject the patient to radiotherapy which is the application of energy to the cells and cells get affected by the field of energy. Therefore, a negative thought will affect cells in the body. And mind you, the cells are the building blocks of a body, and are intelligent. It is necessary to have healthy cells to have a healthful life. Diseases are the result of changes or distortions in cellular physiology and in some cases, their biology. It may be due to many factors, no doubt, but changes

in cells are the root cause of diseases which could happen due to the vibrations caused by negative thoughts. Though we know the pathophysiology of infectious diseases, we have only rudimentary knowledge about lifestyle diseases. Moreover, most suicides can be attributed to negative thinking. That may be the other end of the spectrum. But no one can deny that negative thoughts cause negative vibrations which adversely impact health eventually manifesting in lifestyle diseases.

So, we know that in order to reach a state of spirituality, we need to dissociate from ego, greed, envy, the sense of possessiveness etc. Many philanthropists and organisations do remarkable service to society, but one must remain cautious against developing an ego of superiority on achieving success as it may add to one's ego and arrogance. That once again would be detrimental, and one must guard against developing such an attitude. Ego leads to the development of a sense of attachment. "Attachment signifies an act in which ego claims to be the owner of the object it possesses."[37] Anyone who develops a sense of attachment will suffer grief on the loss of the object to which he was attached. Stronger the attachment, greater will be the grief on its loss. One should not allow his ego to take control of his mind. Egoism is a subtle pollutant and is not easy to get rid of. It distorts straight thinking and blocks the true value of a thought. When unchecked, ego is like a whirlpool drawing thought into its swirling depth which disrupts the mental tranquillity.

Desire and Spirituality

At this point, it is necessary to understand that desire is the element that stands between the man and his effort to obtain a state of tranquillity, an essential part of spirituality. Desire generates from an individual ego. It may not be possible to detach from ego completely, but it is always possible to practice a haircut (in the parlance of share market dealings) and lower the quanta of desire, to finally extirpate the deleterious part of it. The objectivity of Mind plays a vital role in the effort to diminish and suppress desire. Mind you desire is one of the fundamental qualia of individual nature; it is a natural fruit on the tree of the personal ego. One day, someone raised a very pertinent question to me, "How one can jettison ego in life?" One can get over anger, deceitfulness, envy etc., but not the 'ego of being'. On one hand, ego of being is crucial to life as without it, man may not be able to achieve many feats. A soldier may not be able to give his best in a battle, commanders of military units may not be able to discipline troops and draw respect from the ranks, a fighter pilot may not be able to succeed against enemy (as he or she could have) in a dogfight. But on the other, it is the fountainhead of all different types of ego—the ego of superiority, ego of knowledge, ego of power and position in society, etc. One may conquer the ego of power, position etc., and control desire but cannot completely extirpate the ego of being as it is the most fundamental quale of life. Similarly, desire is an essential attribute of human nature because, without desire, progressive life may not be possible. It may not be possible to achieve advancement in the material world, not even in the spiritual gains. One may not be able to excel in studies and scientific research. 'Self-esteem' is an important personal attribute without which one may not have the drive to excel, and desire is the drive to self-esteem. If a person extinguishes desire, he jeopardises his self-esteem. Many philosophers, writers, saints, and seers advise to destroy ego and desire, but it is a piece of advice that is impossible to accomplish. We are dealing with earthly human nature and not an ethereal being. Even the primordial source, call it Brahman or whatever, is not completely devoid of desire. It may not have other human attributes but it has the desire to manifest.

The fundamental nature of desire is "to enter the minds of all living beings in an invisible form, and by creating desire you will assist in the activities of procreation forever . . . I have assigned, Kama, Lord of Desire, the honourable task of facilitating creation."[38] This was the parting advice that Brahman gave to his mind-born child, Kama. The embedding quality of Kama can be gauged looking at the following illustrative passages from Kalidas's famous epic poem in Sanskrit, Abhigyan Shakuntalam[39]:

1. O' god who churns men's mind, how is it that your weapons claimed to be flowers are so sharp?
2. The moon's rays pregnant with ice shoots darts of fire, and your arrows are tipped with the hardest adamant.

Therefore, it may not be advisable to teach extinguishing the fire of desire; the light within, as it may be altruistic but not practical, and certainly against the sustainability of creation. However, all will agree that the flame has to be kept under control so that it does not burn the house.

The mantra is that desire may be allowed to bloom. It must be kept under control to attaining better and more meaningful material world and spiritual life. Let not the flowers of desire ripen to poisonous fruits. In other words, it may not be possible to eliminate desire, perhaps that may not be proper as life advances fruitfully on the plank of desire. But it is always advisable to keep it under control so that its harmful effects are arrested. Lust dwells in three places, the mind, the senses, and the intellect. We must understand what is relevant in life is not the desire as such but its lustful effects. The only way to deal with this scourge is to control its harmful effects. That is where self-control (knowing your mind) is relevant!

The deeper layer of any religion is spirituality because the essence of any religion, as stated earlier, is to take humanity to a higher plane of existence. That can happen only when one keeps desire and ego under control and imbibe the spirit of a religion-the spirituality. Looking outward is natural but looking inside is rather difficult. One needs to be looking inwards to know his mind to control desire. Only then one may be able to overcome its negative effects.

Inner Self and the Exterior World

Let's take a closer look at what comprises the 'self'. What is the selfish versus egalitarian attitude? Imagine yourself at the centre of interrelatedness and every other relationship at the periphery. Your concern and interest of any kind will generate from your individuality and gravitate towards you. This element of self will be heavily pronounced in your thoughts and actions. Whereas, if you place the world at the centre and yourself at the periphery of interrelatedness, your thoughts and actions will primarily have an element of concern for the world, and the universe at large. In Figure 2, you can see that interrelatedness is a two-way path. Self and the outside. Internal and external vibes travel continuously between the self and the world outside. We may understand it as the efferent and afferent flow, akin to the central nervous system. Thick arrows depict the stronger efferent flow, and the thin arrows depict the weak afferent flow. The efferent flow will always be stronger than the afferent since efferent impulse is capable of bringing about effectual changes in the targeted organ.

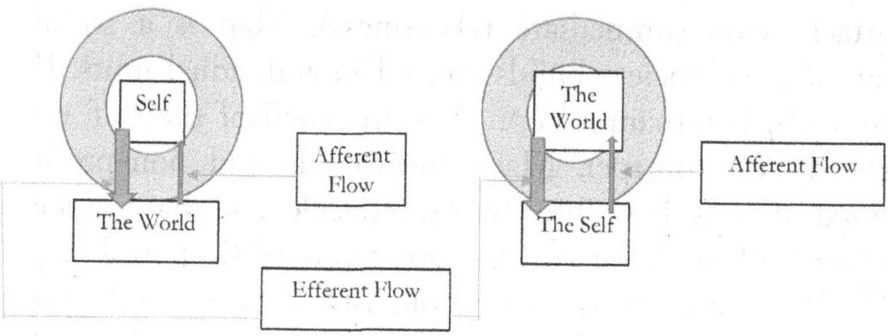

Figure 2: Interrelated Self and the World

Where the self is at the centre, the efferent flow from the self to the periphery will be stronger than the afferent flow from the periphery to the self at the centre, and just the opposite in case where the world is at the centre. Therefore, keeping the world-concern at the centre will be more egalitarian and altruistic, as against keeping the self at the centre which will be selfish. In this context, one may recapitulate life in an Indian joint family which consist of several family members living together.

Whatever may be the advantages and disadvantages, one thing stands out clearly that individuals who grow up in such an environment develop an egalitarian attitude as they don't form a concentrated bond or attachment with a single family member. That is why, for them, feeling a part of a community and being accepted in an alien social milieu is much easier compared to an individual who has grown up in a nuclear family. Therefore, one must extend his thoughts beyond direct relationships and capture the broader domain of interrelatedness extrapolated to the world at large. A mother or a father may remain deeply attached to their children as that is natural. But greater happiness may be in store for those who rise above such attachments (immediate relatedness). Man is a social animal, and society builds around its individual units. If individuals remain cocooned in the shell of the self, no society can prosper. Many individuals and non-profit organisations have broken the shackle and have done remarkable social service. Corporate Social Responsibility (CSR) is also in that direction. But still, we find that the root cause of people not caring for anything beyond their egoistic envelop is the sense of attachment and possessiveness.

Divinity and Human Endeavour

This apart, all of us lay everything on the divine, and consider human endeavour of lesser, or no importance. We have two ends of the spectrum: one is that all doings are the will of Almighty, and the other is that whatever happens is man's doing. Religious pundits will say that things happen with the will of Almighty, but a materialist will always say that changes take place in one's life through human endeavour. This contradiction will remain forever and there will always be a conflict between man's free will and God's will! Therefore, it will be incorrect to leave everything on the divine shoulders and sit back doing nothing. As discussed, ego is a strong bind on the human mind, but man with rationality and discerning ability can overcome the ego-limitations. Man has the potential to reach a higher state through spirituality but is generally prevented by his selfish nature, greed, and deceitful conduct. Spiritually enlightened people (saints and seers) can show the way, but primarily, it is an individual exercise, and one must experience the steps himself. Spirituality is not a part of any school curriculum where one learns alphabets nor is it taught in a seminary. It is the outcome of individual development. Love all, hate none is the basis of spirituality. Many also try the religious route to reach enlightenment. We go to our temples, churches, and mosques and pay obeisance with spread out palms or with folded hands and ask for a blessing or a boon. But the fact is that more than 99 per cent of what people seek in temples is mundane—a windfall, success in examinations, well-being of a sick person, beget children, etc. Such mundane wishes are well within man's capability, and there is no reason to involve the divine for them. One may assume that having a child may not be within man's reach, but a closer examination will lead one to conclude that this too is well within human capability. For example, limiting the human population is well within man's capability.

Thus, it is evident that most prayers have a sense of self-attachment. You will hardly find anyone praying without a selfish motive. What we need to realise here is that the Almighty has already given so much . . . a life, a discerning mind with rationality, and free will to choose his action.

And it is the human endeavour that takes man to a higher plane of existence. For a religious person fate and destiny are more important than what he can do! This way religion acts as a dampener to dreams and aspiration.

Religion, as discussed, is by and large sectarian and parochial and cannot provide a secular platform to achieve enlightenment. That is why in every religion, we find that concept of spiritualism developed as a natural phenomenon. The development of *the Sufi* sect in Islam is a brilliant example. Baha'i faith is another example of humanity seeking spiritualism. Development of bhakti-cult in Hinduism as a natural cascade is yet another example of people trying to reach a higher plane of existence through spirituality. In many ways, the man has devised over the last few centuries to side-line religious doctrines and rituals in favour of spiritualism. Religion is the manifest, and spirituality is the essence, just like body and soul. One may not visit a temple but be spiritual, and at the same time, remain relevant to religion. Spirituality is not to discard a religion but to go beyond. Social divide based on caste and religion, wealth, and social status are real in a material world. However, being spiritual is to go beyond all these stratifications.

vi. Genes: Deterministic of Life

The historicity of genetics has an ancient origin and has attracted many sentient minds including philosophers and scientists. In ancient Greece, Pythagoras (C-530 BCE) postulated that it was the male semen that carried the genetic information and that the pregnant woman acted as an incubator for it. His view was that the male semen collected all information from different parts of the body by absorbing the mystical vapour from each part. Females were only for maturing and providing nourishment to the child and did not contribute to the transfer of genetic code. But his hypothesis and ideas could not explain how then the female body developed into a completely different anatomical and physiological entity since the male body could not have female parts to collect the feminine code. Later, Aristotle, more than a century after (C-380 BCE), rejected the notion that heredity was carried exclusively in male semen.[40] Charak (C-300 BCE), the ancient Indian physician, also known as the father of medicine in India, says that the following four factors determine the characteristic of a child:

1. Those from the mother's reproductive material
2. Those from father's sperm
3. Those from the diet of the pregnant mother
4. Those accompanying the soul which enters the foetus

He further says that these four factors create sixteen further factors of which karma of parents and the soul determine predominant attributes in the child.[41] Charak received his medical education at the University of Taxila, a renowned university in ancient India. He believed in the doctrine of 'prevention is better than cure', which, to this day, remains the critical pillar of healthcare practice. From the factors he described, it is apparent that he believed in the contribution of both father and mother. When he talks of other factors such as diet, he mainly implies environmental factors having an impact as well. Of course, in line with Hindu philosophy, he also certainly believed in the influence of karma and soul. His work and teachings are contained in *Charak Samhita* which is considered to be an opus of medical science and also forms the basis of Ayurveda.

Over time, science has made much progress and scientists have tried to unravel the mystery of the living world through genetic mapping. Hugo de Vries (1848-1935), a Dutch botanist and one of the first geneticists, said, *"Just as physics and chemistry go back to molecules and atoms, the biological sciences have to penetrate these units [genes] in order to explain ... the phenomenon of the living world ...*"[42] We now know that genes are unique. Meaning that the genetic structure of one species cannot develop another species. Generally, the genetic transfer is vertical, i.e., from the parents to the offspring. Even if a foetus develops in a surrogate mother, the morphological resemblance will still be of the biological parents. The physiological and psychological development will be affiliated to the biological parents. No doubt, diet and environmental stress may impact the fetal growth but it will not impact genotype but only the phenotype development (the expressed behaviour of an organism).

To summarise, genes are specific to anatomical, psychological, and physiological phenomenal outcome in the living world. At the same time, it is essential to understand that the environment also impacts the phenomenal outcome of a species. So, the overall outcome for a living organism can be said to be a combination of genetic plus environmental factors. Impact of unpredictable environmental factors was one of the reasons why eugenics (selective human breeding) was discarded as it could never give the desired outcome since science may control genetic configuration, but cannot have desired control on the interaction between the individual and the environment. Much before the German Nazis thought of the idea of eugenics, it was widely advocated in many countries, including the United Kingdom, the USA, and Canada. The original progenitor of the idea was Plato, the Greek philosopher (428/427 BCE).[43] The outcome of eugenics is highly unpredictable especially in the development and growth of a human child. Moreover, the very idea of eugenics for humans militates against the fundamental values of human rights and ethics, at least in the professed principle of negative eugenics (forced sterilisation). One can, of course, argue that if selective breeding can succeed in animals then why not apply it to humans? It is best to leave this discussion at this point as it does not relate strictly to the topic of our concern.

* * *

When we look at the seminal work of Charles Darwin which describes the mechanism of natural selection, one may start wondering how all the different species may have developed? A possible explanation for it can be found in the science of genetic mutation. Genetic mutation is a biological phenomenon obtainable by genetic engineering (intentionally changing the genetic code and configuration) or naturally due to environmental stress. All of these can affect gene expression. Genes have the inherent potential of dynamic expression. In the scientific history of genetics, one finds two schools of thought. One is that the epigenetic factors through DNA methylation often modify gene expression. That is how science explains the physical and psychological differences in subsequent generations. The mutated expression may take a few generations to be evident as changes in the gene expression do not take place instantaneously but over generations. That essentially is the process of evolution. It will take generations for the genes to acquire heritable genotype changed expression. Supposing expression of mutated genes takes place every 10-15 generations. For human species, this may be anything between 500-1000 years, whereas for bacteria, it may be within a few hours as most bacterial flora regenerates every 20-40 minutes or so. That is how bacterial and viral epidemics and pandemics are caused frequently by mutated variants, that include Ebola, SARS, bird flu, swine flu, as well as the Novel Coronavirus (Covid-19). The second school of thought is that it is only the genes that express both the genotype and phenotype. But it does not explain the impinging effects of the environment responsible for phenotype changes.

We know that genes are deterministic to physical appearance and mental construct. We also know that an individual's appearance cannot be precisely the same as parents based on two counts; the first being that an embryo is a result of the genetic conjugation from both the father and the mother, and second due to different environmental impact. Similarly, physiological and psychological attributes will also not be the same as that of the father or mother. In short, we know that physical appearance and other attributes are likely to be much in common in an offspring and his or her parents, but what we do not know is the cause of differences in the gross personality projection. These differences over generations play an important role otherwise the human inheritance tree would ripen to the same physical, physiological, and psychological fruits. The regenerative factory of all living species does not produce the same prototypes like a toy industry rolling out the same type of doll in multitude. We know that energy cannot be destroyed, experiences, which are also energy monads, cannot be destroyed upon the death of a being. There is a continuous change taking place in the evolution of body and mind from generation to generation, apart from genetic changes. While discussing the transient nature of the universe, A.L. Basham (1914-1986), professor of Asian Civilisation at the Australian National University, Canberra, asserts that in the Buddhist theology, "The universe is transient . . . The old man is . . . not the same person as the baby in arms. At every instant, the old man vanishes, and a new man caused by the first comes into being."[44] Thus, there is a continuous change, and that is evolution!

From the discussion above, we know that genetic and epigenetic influences are the cause of similarity as well as of dissimilarity. Genetic manipulation may lead to different variants in a species. It may be good or bad depending upon whether it is supportive or destructive to a species. "The cells with the same genetic programming could be reproduced divided, transplanted, and so on. Another animal or human being could be produced . . . through cloning. What would then happen to personal identity then?"[45] A very pertinent question in contrariety. The explanation of inheritable differences may lie in two factors that we have discussed (genetic and epigenetic factor), that is the effects of environmental factors which starts right from the childhood and continues throughout the life of a person.

A child is devoid of layers of individuation (a process through which one acquires a uniqueness) at its birth, and perhaps, during the initial few years as well. After birth, a child gets exposed to environmental and other factors shaping up its mind and personality. That way, its perception, feelings, predilection, and tendencies will be unique and individualistic. However, even the impact of environmental factors alone cannot fully explain the differences. There is another more important reason for the differences among individuals and even siblings. This difference may be perhaps due to the spirit or soul that each person harbours and somewhat shapes a personality, albeit partially, but it casts a strong influence. So, we can say that each person's outlook will not only be based upon inherited genes, not only on the external factors but also on the embodied soul.

Life is experiential and the environment is an educator. However, this experience has two parts: the first one being what is presented, and the other what one gains from it. What one wrings out of an experience will depend upon one's personality, his outlook, his resolve, as well as his mental construct. The outcome of experiences will be different in different individuals since no two persons have the same personality, the same outlook, or the same mental construct. Personality includes inherent characteristics, traits, and tendencies which modulate individual behaviour. Take external stress, for example. Stress may be common, but the mental turmoil one may feel would be an individualised reactive feeling. Two individuals may face the same stress of the same order, but one just ignores it and moves on, while another gets highly stressed and bogged down. The interesting part here to note is that the same quanta and qualia of a stressful situation may as well produce different grades of felt impact in an individual at different time and space. So even though personality appears to be a permanent template, changes do occur in different circumstances and time. It would be incorrect to assume that individual behaviour patterned over a particular personality will prevail for the whole life. There are innumerable examples where the core nature (the personality template) of an individual has undergone remarkable change due to an event or changed circumstances.

A crucial cause for the sustainability of life can be found in the way genes (the root of every living being) retain the previous codes to impact the development of new life. Inherited genes act as a repository of past lives and a recorder of the present. When a child is born, the genetic code of parents is automatically transplanted. And as discussed, apart from genes, environmental factors also impact the physical and mental development. However, an important question to consider here is whether environmental factors can get carried into genes and influence the next generation? Recently, researchers have come out with the suggestion that the effects of the environmental stress, generally known as epigenetic factors, piggyback on the genes and have a defining role in fetal development. It has now become evident that the impact of life experiences can be passed on to the next generation through epigenetic factors as well. Maybe that is how differences appear from one generation to another. The environment during the life of my father and mother were different than what I face today and will be different in the life of my children and grandchildren. However, a word of caution here—the science of epigenetic influence is presently in infancy but appears reasonably plausible.

Much research is ongoing in genetics, including genetic engineering. Genetic science is a distinct field and is not within the scope of this book. Suffice to say that not only the genetic code but also epigenetic impressions are heritable. These two together find expression in the subsequent generations. Moreover, mutation is the most critical factor in the evolution of species because without genetic variations, perhaps millions of living species may not have evolved. And in this context, one cannot ignore the significance of heritable epigenetic factors.

2
Mind-Body Complex

i. Part I

Let me clarify that the mind-brain complex may be taken as the same as mind-body complex since the brain is a part of the body. It may be necessary to mention here that soul, spirit, life energy, and mind may be subtly different, but all are ethereal elements conjoined with a living body. The distinction between body and the mind has a metaphysical, or religious origin, as brought out by Bertrand Russell: "The distinction between mind and matter . . . has a religious origin, and began as the distinction between body and soul . . . the Orpheus proclaim himself as the child of earth, from earth comes the body and from heaven the soul."[46] The macrocosm of a body of a living species is nothing but the aggregated flora and fauna borrowed from nature meticulously arranged with intelligent design. But it is the spirit or life energy that makes us think and confabulate, gather experiential knowledge and wisdom to live a fruitful life.

Knowledge and Wisdom

The template of Mind may have a divine origin but not

the modifications, additions, and alterations. Mental development never reaches a finality. There is no limit to the plasticity of mind; it remains malleable till death. We gather a lot of information interacting with nature and surroundings. Environment and the surroundings keep changing, and so does the individual mind. Impressions are stacked and used to collect more and more information about the world we live in. The brain is an important part of the body in knowledge gathering. And at every stage of knowledge gathering, the mind undergoes modifications; it changes. Take, for example, academic education. It is incremental. Once a student gathers some knowledge, he uses this knowledge to collect more knowledge. A child first learns the alphabets, then starts to form words out of the alphabets. With higher education, one may become a scientist, a philosopher, or a doctor. These are stages of acquiring incremental knowledge. Knowledge gathering is progressive, so is the wisdom but at a different plane. Knowledge gathering is a function of the brain whereas development of the mind is intellectual. Knowledge and wisdom are closely interconnected but bear different connotation. Knowledge is what you learn whereas wisdom is what you gain out of it. Every person who is knowledgeable may not be wise as learning is required to be mulled, masticated, and crushed in the mental quern-stone to obtain wisdom. It follows therefore that your developed mental attitude has an overriding influence in the development of wisdom. The apps of knowledge-gathering and development of mind are interlinked but not the same. Knowledge is only the first step to gain wisdom. It does not always convert to wisdom.

Therefore, it will be a folly to understand that it is the brain that gives us wisdom. It is the mind that empowers us with wisdom. But since the brain and the mind are closely interlinked, we feel that brain is the seat of the mind. Whenever we think of 'Mind' our thoughts naturally turn to our brain. So, there is a natural tendency to place the mind with the brain. But the reality may be different. Irrefutable evidence of the seat of mind continues to remain unknown. We discuss this aspect in the succeeding paragraph:

Seat of Mind

The riddle philosophers and scientists are yet to solve is the seat of the mind in the body. Does it lie in the anatomical brain or the heart? Or is it always floating in space? Earlier philosophers thought it resided in the heart of vertebrates and other animals, including the human species. However, now, most believe that it has a connection with the brain, whether it resides there or not is debatable. That is why philosophers have coined a term: 'Mind-body or 'Mind-brain' complex. To some, it may appear that the mind is a separate feature. There is no denying that the mind is not a part of the brain, but it is also true that it somehow remains connected with it. The mind may not reside only in the brain as many bodily functions take place without its direct involvement. For example, the autonomic and cellular functions. Thus, we can deduce that the mind must reside in every element of the body, even in the billions of cells the body has. Cells may not have a brain, but they have a mind. In its mind, every cell is conscious and aware of what it is doing and why it is doing it. The rushing of white blood cells to the site of a wound or an abscess is the scientific expression of healing. But why such action should take place and how the cells are attracted towards the injury or a sore is not found in scientific pursuance.

Obviously, they have a mind. In the same way, brainless species exhibit afferent and efferent mental flow, which is receiving input and directing an action, respectively. The mindful life process transgresses the need to have a brain. It directs the species what to do in a given circumstance. Through efferent flow, it directs microbes towards acquiring resistance or anatomical shield (vegetative bacteria transforming to spores) as a safety measure; and look for food for sustenance, etc., after having received input through the afferent flow.

Another example would be when we have a scary nightmare. We wake up with a feeling of anxiety, pounding heart, and sweating body. What happens is that the scary thing in the horrific dream engineers a body reaction without you being consciously aware of it. Thus, we can conclude that reactive intelligence is not outside but within, and it is not dependent on your woken awareness. Therefore, it may be futile to search for the seat of mind in any particular part of the body as it is all-pervasive. It is the sentient vapour rising out of every cell in our body, manifesting and functioning as the mind. It engineers our thinking, our actions, and our feelings.

To illustrate this point, it may be necessary to take the help of a fantasy. Many may have seen the serial *Star Trek*. It is shown there that a body can be transported to an alien planet. The subject person stands in a cubicle. After all the information has been scanned and gathered, he is transported (replicated) in an atomised state on another planet. The idea may appear weird and highly hypothetical at present but is a distinct possibility, if not in the near, maybe in a distant future. A few hundred years ago, no one could imagine that one could see a person on TV screen sitting thousand miles away in real-time. But this is possible now. You can see not only the person, but also his anatomical features, the colour of his tie, and also determine when he blinks in near real-time frame. Similarly, who knows that in another hundred years, one may be able to transport a human body not only anatomically but also physiologically to another planet. By this method, one may be able to transport biological features cell by cell but not the mind if the mind is not inherent in each cell. As growth takes place, intelligent cells gain experience through external factors and human-induced stress, and modify accordingly. Therefore, they are peculiar. We know that cells in our body regularly die and are replaced with new cells. These new cells are a replica of the old ones. And in replication, they inherit the original mindfulness. That is how the replicated cells behave precisely in the same manner as the previous ones. Thus, it is reiterated that mind is universally inherent in each part, each cell of the body.

With this interjection, we return to the fantasy of *Star Trek*. It may be possible to create a biological replica, but what about the mental attributes? If we go by substance dualism (or even property dualism), where the mind is considered a separate entity and not an inherent part of the cells, the biological replica will be devoid of a mind. Without a mind, the organic body will be of no use. On the other hand, if the mind is inherent in every cell, transporting the body will also mean transporting the mind, lock, stock, and barrel! However, for this, science will have to discover measures to transgress the limiting factor of the Einsteinian theory that no physical object can move faster than light. But here the contemplation is not any physical object but non-physical transmission materialising into physical at the destination. If mankind has to realise and discover the multiverse from close quarters within a reasonable time frame, it may be necessary to transgress the limitations of speed. To realise the esoteric, one may have to cross the limits of the human brain and open the mind to connect with the divine!

Returning back to the physiological aspect of mind-brain, or mind-body relationship, the application of mind through the brain is relevant only when the mind is associated with the body. A thought occurring in mind will be of use only when it is related to the brain, and brain activity will be of use only when it activates the body, either the physical or the mental. Thus, there are three factors in the thought-to-action process:

1. The first factor is the thought itself. Every thought has a quality and even if the thought is similar, its perceived nature will differ in different individuals as no two minds are the same. The nature of a particular thought on the same perceptive cue will follow the nature of the individual mind and hence will be different.
2. The second factor is the brain. The capacity and nature of brain of different individuals will be different and therefore, the perception and action will differ.
3. The third factor is the body due to which the action will depend upon the physical qualities of the body.

Mind to Bodily Action

The most important factor is thoughts originating in

the mind. All other actions take place thereafter. It is an everyday experience that thoughts generate continuously in the human mind, even during periods of inactivity. Many times, one cannot put the finger on the origin as many thoughts are triggered by emotions. Emotion (discussed later) is an integral part of the mind but is not necessarily contained in the brain. The brain has three major faculties: the autonomic, the somatic, and the reflex nervous systems. Somatic actions are through the brain. Most of our conscious action is directed by the somatic part of our brain. It is not easy to discern the priori of a bodily action at a given point in time and space because it is the mind that triggers an action through the brain, and not only that the brain directs it. Many times, we are not aware of why we did something. The state of the mind at a given point in time is sometimes not predictable. Autonomic, as evident, works on its own, without us being conscious of it. This includes the cardiac, respiratory (at rest), and digestive systems. On the other hand, reflex actions originate out of the conditioning of the mind, and they occur instantaneously. Immediate withdrawal from a flame and stiffening of striated muscles when expecting a physical blow are examples of reflex actions. Long back when I was in the NCC we were practising rifle-parade. The instructor was shouting orders. The cadet on my right was perhaps overenthusiastic and manoeuvred his rifle with force to place it on his shoulder. In the process, the butt of rifle hit me on the face. Fortunately, it hit over my masticating muscle (the masseter muscle) which was already in contraction during the manoeuvre I was doing, simultaneously. Though the hit was strong enough to loosen some of my teeth nothing much happened as the muscle was already stiffened. Thus, reflex actions are highly protective.

Intellectual Mind

Therefore, there is much more to know about the mind-brain complex. Science has mostly established, what is anatomy and physiology of the brain, what is psychology and psychiatry, but what constitutes mind, and its interrelatedness with brain still remains a puzzling riddle. It is noteworthy that intellect controls, influences, and guides the functionality of the mind. The intellectual property of a person is based on various factors. Some may be genetic, but mostly it is experiential. Western thinkers and philosophers consider mind and intellect to be the same. If mind and intellect are the same, then such debate on mind and brain may be pointless. However, in Sanatana Hindu tradition, these two are viewed separately. In Samkhya philosophy, *mahat* is the term used to denote the infinite universal mind that endows ego. In turn, the ego generates *mana* (the inner self), *buddhi* (intellect), *and ahamkara* (ego), followed by sense and action faculties. Thus, it is evident that Indian philosophers considered all these varied qualia of mind; intellect being just one of them. Thus, the mind and intellect are not the same. What we usually understand by the intellect is the developed wisdom of a mental faculty. Whether it is present in all living species to the same degree may be questionable, but Intelligent mind is present in all living species, even in creatures without a brain. Brainless creatures like unicellular organisms, bacteria, cells in our body, etc., do not have a brain but have a mind. These do not need a brain as there are no action organs to be activated. Meaning that such organisms do not have arms and legs to activate and hence there is no requirement to have neurons, axions, and nerve fibres.

However, all vertebrates, including human beings, need and have a brain as action organs cannot be activated otherwise. We cannot transmit action-oriented thoughts, without a brain. We can find a close analogy in the history of the development of automobiles in the reverse order. Decades ago, it may have been unthinkable to have a car without a clutch pedal. However, now with the automatic vehicles, the clutch plate is simply not needed as there is no need for a gear system. Thus, a function that was essential earlier stands eliminated. We can reverse the sequence and imagine that we had a gearless vehicle earlier (similar to organisms without a brain), and now we have vehicles with gears.

Conscious Awareness and Cognition

Having discussed the intelligent mind in all living species we now discuss the conscious awareness, knowledge and wisdom, and cognition of objects. Two things come into play in the sphere of knowledge gathering (to obtain intellectual platform), and the surroundings and the individual mind. Our sense perception establishes a connection with the object and the information is transmitted to the brain and then to mind where it is analysed and a course of action determined. One cannot understand the surroundings only through perception; conception is also required which won't be possible without consciousness. Consciousness is a mental attribute through which we experience the state of awareness. We are aware of ourselves through individual consciousness. Every external object also has consciousness. A person in a beautiful garden experiences joyous awareness not only through his individual consciousness but also with the consciousness of the garden. To explain it further, let us consider the following scenario. There are two friends who take morning walks in a park regularly and thereafter sit on a bench and chit-chat. But one day, for some reason, they enter into an argument and are not in a talkative mood. This shift will affect the self-awareness of both individuals. Thus, the state of our self-awareness changes with what is around. David R. Hawkins (1927-2012), an authority on consciousness and spirituality, says in his book, *The Eye of the I*, "The inner sense of reality is bestowed by the self on the 'outer' surroundings . . . the sense of realness is therefore a projection of consciousness by the self, originating from the self."[47] This may appear confusing as the self and surroundings appear to remain the same. But one perceives the surrounding with intellect and the in-built nature of the mind, which differs with time and space in the same individual. If you are hungry, a delectable dish will bring out salivary secretions, but if your stomach is full, perhaps you will just look at the food and move on. Jesse E. Gordon, an American author, says in his book, *Personality and Behaviour*, "When an individual is hungry, the response associated with eating tend to be high because some of the cues to which these responses are attached . . . are already present and tend to elicit drive related response."48

In order to be captured in the mental frame, an object has to appear in a perceptive field of our sense organs. We see sunlight in only one colour, and at maximum, we can see seven colours with a prism. There may be many more colours outside our perceptive field which our sense organs are unable to capture. Similarly, our ears can comfortably hear sounds within a range of 20-80 decibel, there may be many more sounds in the universe outside our perceptible range. Furthermore, it is the mind that activates the object. 'Eyes see what mind knows' is a common proverb our teachers used to tell us in the medical school when we failed to see poring through the microscope the microbial the teacher wanted us to see. You see with your eyes, understand with your mind, but evaluate an object with your inner consciousness. To understand this better, let us look at another scenario. You are walking in a forest with a botanist friend. You may not be interested in the flora, but your botanist friend surely has an affinity for it. Your eyes will not focus on any plant as your mind is not interested. But your botanist friend will focus his gaze on rare plants as his mind looks for a botanical rarity. In this case, the object is there but fails to attract your attention, but the same object attracts the attention of your botanist friend. The object and the mind interact based on the interests the mind has. In other words, unless the mind activates an object, the intellect does not come into play and the object is not cognised in its complete detail. Therefore, it is perfectly alright to subsume that the object gets activated by the mind. To summarise, through conscious-perceptive awareness, an interaction takes placc whereby the object is perceived by sense organ and conceived by inner senses, resulting in a physical act or an imbued feeling. And even though the object may remain the same, its conception will differ with each individual as each individual possesses a unique mind. Similarly, any abstraction cannot sustain on its own and form a mental picture unless it is assimilated and analysed in the individual mind. Thus, cognition can be defined as ". . . the mental action or process of acquiring knowledge and understanding through thought, experience, and senses. It includes intellectual functions and processes such as attention, the formation of knowledge, memory . . . judgment, and evaluation."[49]

Mental construct is dynamic and keeps changing with time and space. A person will perceive an external cue differently at a different time and place. It is not the quale of the object that determines the object as such, but the conceptive mind that identifies the object. A rose flower is determined to be a rose flower through an analytical examination in our mind. Our mind analyses the object and compares it with stored imagery and concludes that it indeed is a rose flower. Baruch Spinoza puts it succinctly, "I say conception rather than perception, for the name perception seems to point out that the mind is passive to the object, while conception seems to express an action of the mind."[50] The mind may not have any physical connection with the brain, but it has an abstract relation with it. The mind generates ideas that result in an action, mental or physical. With its emotional features, ego, knowledge, and wisdom, mind generates action-oriented thoughts and feelings.

Power of Spoken Words

The mind is a powerful attribute, and spoken words are integral feature of the mind, not only in the didactic language but also in the sermons delivered by an enlightened person. Saints and seers were the progenitors of great ideas that influenced masses in a defining way. They were able to convince the masses about an idea by exporting positive energy through their spoken words. Their words had tremendous power to influence the audience. A narrative stated by a common man may not have the same effect on the masses as a sermon given by a saint or seer who has garnered wisdom and spiritual power through study, penance, and mediation. But one may wonder how spoken words can have so much power. We must realise that spoken words are energy variants and carry inherent strength a person may have gathered through knowledge, wisdom, and purity of mind. A lecture by an ordinary teacher will not have the same effect on students as one given by an expert in the field who teaches not only with the knowledge about the subject but also with a deep conviction in what he teaches. Therefore, the same words may have different effects on the listener depending upon the person who speaks it. Sri Sathya Sai Baba (1926-2011), Indian spiritual guru and a philanthropist, says, *"When words referring to worldly situations have such transforming effect on the mind of man, certainly words conveying spiritual and elevated meaning will help in cleansing and correcting the mind of man."*[51] Prophets of yesteryears were able to connect to the vast ocean of consciousness of the cosmos and capture profound understanding about life, human suffering, eternal joy, etc. That is how they were able to impact their audience in a defining way. Adi Shankara, Swami Vivekananda, and Ramakrishna Paramhansa are few examples from the Indian history who wielded this power. In fact, every civilisation can boast of innumerable philosophers and preachers in every epoch who can be said to have a link with the cosmic consciousness.

Mind-Brain Interrelatedness

Science may have gathered much knowledge about the human body but not enough about the mind. The connecting bond between mind and brain remains an enigma. Philosophers and scientists from ancient times have pored over the issue without evolving a clear physical or metaphysical explanation. There are two terms relevant to the topic (propounded by Rene Descartes) of the mind-matter complexity. One is 'substance dualism' and the other is 'property dualism'. Metaphysics of substance dualism is easy to understand as it posits the concept in which two different things combine somehow. Whereas, to understand property dualism, it is necessary to realise that the same thing can manifest differently with distinct qualia while retaining its originality. Water, when heated, produces steam. Water is the original substance; it retains its originality, that is its molecular configuration. It does not change with the physical change. When steam is cooled, it reverts to the original state of water.

Rene Descartes (1596-1650 CE) actively advanced the idea that the mind interacted with the body through the pineal gland, a proposition agreed by some but hotly contested by many. Plato asserted that the soul (the mind) is temporarily associated with the body (the matter) and the material world. Aristotle thought the soul, a property exhibited by the body got destroyed when the body perished. Thomas Aquinas (1225-1274 CE) believed that the mind and the body were one, referring to the mind as the soul. He further asserted that the soul persisted after the death of the body despite their unity. Many philosophers and theorists in the recent past (19th and 20th century), such as Immanuel Kant, Thomas Huxley, Karl Popper, and John Searle, put their thoughts on the mind-body problem.[52] All of them considered mind separate than the body in one way or the other, but could not define clearly as to how the connection between the two worked. Saints and seers said it was pointless to search for the mind as it was already within and not without. Whichever way we look at the mind-body problem, we find no resolution.

The main problem appears to be the postulate of dualism. Even if we concede to this idea, the discussion does not find a clear direction because the term 'duality' indicates separateness and not togetherness. Whereas the mind may be an innate property of every cell in the body, just like life energy. In the metaphysical contemplation of Indian philosophy, substance and property dualism is briefly explained below:

> Brahman exists in two forms—*Nirguna* and *Sagun*. It is the *Sagun Brahman (purusha)* that interacts with nature *(prakriti)* and manifests. This is the view of Samkhya philosophy (the dvaita concept). This, in simple terms, is substance dualism. But when the revealed (physical or abstract) manifests in a different *avatar* than the original, as Brahman in *Advaita* philosophy, it is property dualism. Brahman, in this case, manifests as soul or mind (life energy) which forms the basis of a living body. In the *Dvaita* concept, *purusha* and *prakriti* are two separate elements and life evolves when they conjoin together. On the other hand, the *Advaita* concept says that *prakriti* cannot be conceived as a separate entity as it is a manifestation of the same cosmic element, Brahman. In both, the originality is neither curtailed nor lost. But in both, the soul or mind acquires different qualia when conjoined with the body, the earthly element. The mind, a resultant phenomenon, evolves with different properties than from where it originated. Just like steam has different properties than water from where it arose.

The Pineal Gland

Let us now discuss the wondrous element of the human psyche, the mind-brain connectivity in little more detail. We wonder as to how the thoughts generating in our mind is transmitted to the brain to activate a corporeal outcome. In the ancient metaphysical confabulation and later scientific deliberations, the mind and its connection with the brain centres around the pineal gland. Ancient Indian philosophers considered it a vestigial remnant of the mythological 'third eye of Lord Shiva.' It is a tiny neuroendocrine gland measuring about five to seven millimetre in length and weighs less than one gram. But surprisingly, it receives profuse blood flow, second only to the kidneys.[53] It is well-known that higher blood flow occurs in a highly active organ. Pineal gland appears to be such an organ. It is situated near the centre of our brain, tucked in between the two hemispheres. Its development takes place in early childhood, maybe up to one to three years, and it remains stable after that. Most vertebrates have a pineal gland. Much literature is available on the possible functions of the pineal gland. However, apart from its role in circadian rhythm (through melatonin which is a hormone produced by it) and control of the endocrine system, not much is known on its other functions.

We do not know for sure if there is a connecting bond between the mind and brain through the pineal gland. And if there is one, we do not know how it works. Answer to this vexed question may not be forthcoming through material science but can be found through metaphysics. Pineal gland corresponds positionally with the vestige of the mythical third eye of Lord Shiva and is also known as the inner eye. A mythical story describes that Lord Shiva's consort, Goddess Parvati, closed his eyes in jest. It resulted in profound darkness in the universe and as a reactionary solution, the third eye of Lord Shiva opened lighting the universe. This mythical anecdote may also be in relation to the conscious and unconscious states of the primordial universe.

During ancient times, philosophers thought that the pineal gland regulated the flow of spirit. The first description and the first speculation about the pineal gland can be found in the voluminous writing of Galen, the Greek physician, surgeon, and philosopher (C 129-216 CE)[54] who spent the majority part of his life in Rome. Galen discussed the pineal gland in the eighth book of anatomical work and named the gland 'pineal' due to its resemblance to pine nuts. He worked to refute an opinion, apparently current at the time, that the pineal gland regulated the flow of psychic pneuma between the middle and posterior brain ventricles.[55] Rene Descartes hypothesised the pineal gland as the principal seat of the soul. Descartes was not only interested in philosophy but also human anatomy and physiology. His conclusions were mostly speculative and hypothetical and not experimentally proven. But his thoughts engineered intense debate and continues to engage the minds of philosophers even today. He argued that the mind and the body though being two different entities were, in fact, interrelated. In the *Treatise of Man*, he suggests that body and soul are two different substances. He aimed first to describe the soul and then the body, separately on its own, and then tried to join these two in order to constitute what is a man. During his lifetime, he wrote about the soul and body but was not able to write about the fusion that resulted in the development of a living body.

Though the role of the pineal gland is yet to be fully established, we may have a postulate or a pseudo hypothesis where a link between the mind (abstract) and the body (corporeal), through our brain (pineal gland) appear probable. The pineal gland in the human brain could be the receiving and transmitting station. It may be something like a transmitting tower that receives input messages and transmits it to the intended recipient. The flow from mind to the pineal gland and then to the intended brain centre could be the efferent flow, whereas stimuli from sense organs to the pineal gland and then to the mind is the afferent flow. The different stages of perceptive awareness in the Hindu tradition are supposedly contained within the seven chakras. The pineal gland is thought to be situated in the sixth chakra—*ajna.* Directly above the *ajna* is the *manas* chakra (a minor chakra) responsible for sending sense perceptions to higher chakra. Philosophers since ancient times have pondered over the question as to how thoughts are transmitted and how perceptions warranting attention and action are gathered in the mental frame. The possible explanation they offer is that a connection does exist between the mind and brain, but 'how' is not elaborated. It remains a matter of conjecture.

Universal and Individual Consciousness

It is evident that individual consciousness is a gift of universal consciousness. Some may argue that since the universe is not a living body, it may not have any consciousness. But consciousness is not a result of material manifestation; instead, the manifestation is the result of consciousness. If there will be no physical universe, the universal consciousness will still be there, waiting to manifest. Consciousness is an abstract state, unlike the brain, which is physical. One cannot see, hold, or dissect consciousness. We know that the universe contains infinite energy. Earlier scientists considered deep space as a void, whereas later, the physical discoveries and metaphysical considerations indicate that space is not void. It is now well established that it is filled with ether. Quantum mechanics, string theory, and many recent scientific hypotheses have established that space is not a dark lagoon where there is no activity but rather consists of oscillating structures which create vibrations. That is why it is said that whatever your mind thinks or conjures should be good if it connects and corresponds with the continuous vibration of the universe. Nikola Tesla (1856-1943), the great inventor who holds about 300 patents in his name, said, *"If you want to find the secrets of the universe, think in terms of energy, frequency, and vibration."*[56] Amazingly, he was way ahead of his time and his profound discovery of alternating current (AC) was brought to practical use after 15 years of the invention. So, when we consider it in the context of the material world, we can see it as the universal consciousness and the material world draws energy from universal consciousness. Most probably, the unconscious mind remains connected to the universal consciousness and that is how greatly concentrated thoughts sometimes reveal profound results. I would like to share a story here to elucidate this fact.

I was born and brought up in a village and had my schooling there. We belonged to a well to do upper middle-class family but always felt the cash crunch, and we did not have the usual luxury items. There was only one clock in the outer room. I used to come to the village during college holidays. Once I was required to get up early in the morning to catch a bus and then a train to my destination. I remember that me and my other siblings would ask the stars to wake us up at a particular time, at 3 or 3:30 a.m. And we used to wake up at the exact time as if the stars stirred us from our sleep. It never failed. However, later I realised that it was not the stars but my unconscious mind that acted upon the suggestions. In the narrated incident, one can see that the unconscious mind coordinated with the universal mind or universal consciousness. This shows that even though the universal mind may not be a part of the body, it remains connected to the individual mind.

Many philosophers also propose the existence of a universal mind or universal consciousness, and that we possess only a tiny part of this universal consciousness. What we possess as the mind is only an infinitesimal part of the vast universal mind. The small lagoon that is the individual mind is connected to the vast ocean through an estuary. One needs to open this estuary to connect to the vast ocean and only then the individual mind can become infinite. Swami Sivananda says, "The cosmic mind is the sum-total of all the minds, and the individual mind is connected to cosmic mind."[57] But everyone does not experience this. It needs focus and dedication to experience the infiniteness of universal consciousness. Individual minds may be a part of the universal consciousness, but when it dwells in a particular living species, it manifests differently and acquires different qualia through its conjugation with matter. Cosmic consciousness is the same for all, and its purity is without any contained *gunas (qualia)*. The earthly ingredient consists of three *gunas—sattvik, rajasik,* and *tamasik.* In other words, a living person is the product of the three unconscious substances called *sattva* (purity), *rajas* (worldliness), and *tamas* (darkness).[58] It is also averred that all these three remain in balance in *prakriti* (nature) until agitated by *purusha*, (cosmic consciousness). It follows, therefore, that each individual mind will be different depending upon which of these *gunas* predominate the mind. Also, the obtained unique personality is not constant; it changes as the balance of these three contained *gunas* in a person also change with time, moment to moment.

The ancient Indian *Charavaka* school did not believe in karma, rebirth, or afterlife, and asserted, "Consciousness is an emergent quale of the body. There is no consciousness in bodily elements, such as earth and or water. But when they are combined in a certain way, consciousness emerges."[59] They believed the intermingling of the four earthly elements as the cause of life and did not subscribe to the postulate of a soul. They argued that water by itself is considered cool and carries ambient temperature. Only when heated, it changes to steam that can generate power to energise machines. The heat was an outside agent added to the water and that is how water acquired a different quality. When cooled, the steam loses its power and once again returns to its original form. Similarly, a living species acquires individual consciousness, changes its qualia from inanimate to animate and upon death to an inanimate which is its original state. However, such precepts lack conviction. It does not explain how an individual mind is constructed and why it differs from individual to individual. If life was that simple, all living species should have been the same, if not in their appearance, at least in their nature, just like vapour from any type of water will bear same properties. That is why the *Charavaka* thought was considered fallacious and hardly favoured by any other school. It was prevalent during 6th to 5th centuries BCE and may have contributed partly to the Buddhist and Jain metaphysical contemplation. Their works are lost and therefore not much can be said about their thoughts and philosophy.

Indian philosopher Vatsayana raises a materialistic proposition: "Consciousness is a quale of the body, for it exists if there is the body and does not exist if there is not the body."[60] Essentially meaning that individual consciousness is a part of the body. He also explains that the body is conscious sometimes, but not all the time. Upon death, the body is no more conscious. That is a universal fact that a dead body is not conscious, but to consider individual consciousness to be a part of the body only may invite counter arguments. An example would be that a person in deep sleep or coma may seem devoid of consciousness but this is not the case as per the available scientific knowledge. As per the teachings of *Advaita Vedanta*, "It is wrong to assume that when there is no object to be revealed, consciousness also ceases to exist."[61]

So even though the mind may or may not be wholly a part of the body, it remains awakened even in a coma. One may say that it is present in ethereal time-space out of the body. Also, just like the body has to remain viable to hold a soul, in the same way, the body has to be healthy to contain a mind. If not, the mind escapes in the time-space arena while retaining its umbilical connection with the body. It comes back if there is a recovery, but upon death, it merges with the universal consciousness from where it came as the body has lost its capability to retain it. To understand this better, we can compare the mind to a flowing stream in the mountains. It has a life as it flows. Now if its flow is blocked by a falling boulder, it will still flow, finding the best alternate route and when the rock is removed, it will regain its original path. A similar thing happens with the human mind when a person goes into a deep coma.

Near-Death Experience

There are many recorded instances of near-death experience (NDE) where on the recovery, the survivor was able to recapitulate its experiences while being in a deep coma. So, if functional awareness is absent in coma as the brain is shut out, it implies that such experiences are not in the realm of conscious awareness. NDE may be one such experience. So the question arises, are there different worlds in the mind-brain relationship, one visible with conscious awareness and the other which is not in the realm of conscious awareness? Other things to consider is that does a consciously aware brain keeps the unconscious repressed and do mystics experience the outside of the realm of awareness by suppressing their consciously aware brain? We are yet to get a definite answer about these queries.

Eben Alexander, a practicing neurosurgeon for decades, was in deep coma for about two weeks after being afflicted with a severe brain infection and recovered. He was in a position to recount his experiences. He had never read about or heard the Hindu spiritual symbol *Aum* before. But after his recovery, he recapitulated that he heard humming sound of *Aum* all over the universe during his ethereal journey (NASA has discovered a continuous humming sound present in space and some believe that when amplified, the sound resembles the sound of *Aum)*. His awareness returned, once the boulder in the flow of mental river got removed. And once he regained health, he was able to relate what he experienced during his unconscious deep coma state. We can see that the mind retained the umbilical connection with the body. Dr Eben Alexander has described his experiences in his book, *Proof of Heaven*. Many have criticised saying it to be a fantasy. However, his recollection of hearing the sound om *'Aum'*—the sacred sound and spiritual icon of Indic religions, which he had never heard nor had any knowledge about it—substantiates the experience being substantive. Subsequently, he has acquired a philosophic attitude and written several books on life, NDE, spirituality, and the afterlife. This is a good example where a scientist turned to spirituality. Many others have narrated NDE which changed their outlook towards life. Therefore, it is not correct to assume that people in a deep coma lose all their consciousness. Somewhere, in the mental cavern, consciousness continues to weave threads.

However, awareness has levels in a direct relevance to consciousness. Consciousness can be said to be the cause, the root-priori, and awareness its product, an extension. A person fully awake and energetic is on the higher plane of conscious awareness. If he is awake but lethargic, perhaps his awareness is at a low ebb. His response and reactions to a stimulus may not be as instantaneous or sharp as the former. A person in deep sleep or coma may also be consciously aware as the mental activities have not stopped completely. In the background, his mind continues to function; only he may not be consciously aware of it. The essential nature of mind is to think, and it will continue to do so even in deep sleep or coma.

Mindful Life Energy

Life energy and the mind are interconnected or perhaps, are the same. Once life energy is infused the mind starts forming. It follows 'all or none' law. Either it is there, or it is not there. There is no quantification. Life energy departs on the death of a living species, so does the mind. Death is nothing but the inability of the body to hold and retain life energy (and the Mind). Mental function is not exclusive to a human being but is present in all living species, including trees and plants. A seed contains life energy in a latent form. It sprouts with the right atmosphere and proper nutrition. It may be lying dormant somewhere until it finds the correct surroundings to grow. Plants and trees uptake nutrients from the soil and ambient air once it starts growing, which requires the intervention of a mind. Otherwise, why should the roots of a growing tree make inroads in a particular direction breaking through hard and rocky soil to seek an underground water source? Why should an emergent tree outgrow the underbrush seeking sunlight? Plants and trees convert sunlight energy into edible energy. There are saprophytes, parasitic, and carnivorous plants. All supposedly have a mind because many functions that plants exhibit cannot happen mindlessly. Similarly, human sperm and ova contain latent life energy which develops into an embryo. Given the right surroundings and nutrition, it takes nourishment from the mother's womb, just like a plant takes water and nutrients from the soil and the atmosphere. There is, however, another important aspect—to retain life energy. A rotten seed will not develop to a plant or tree, howsoever you put water and nutrient, because there is no life energy in it. In other words, its retention is subject to the health of the matter. In a similar way, retention of the mind is subject to the health of the matter.

Inquisitive Mind

There is another aspect of the mind. It keeps asking questions and seeks answers. In short, a mind is inquisitive. If it were not so, perhaps, the scientific history would have remained a clean slate. It is the inquisitive human mind that seeks an answer to the quintessential seminal question as to 'who am I?' It is the inquisitiveness that geared Newton to discover gravity. His mind inquired answer to a simple question as to why the apple fell towards the earth and not fly off in the sky. That was the beginning of Newtonian laws and with that, spatial and celestial theories and hypotheses enriching the scientific knowledge were developed. We all see the sun making daily rounds over the earth and in the earlier time, people believed that the sun rotated around the earth (geocentric belief), which later changed to the heliocentric belief with Galileo's groundbreaking discovery. Though he paid a heavy price for inquisitiveness but it accelerated the scientific advancement. Such great minds were inquisitive and did not blindly believe what they apparently saw. However, there is a flip side to this important feature. Our mind may be inquisitive, but at the same time, it is bureaucratic and resists change. Fortuitously, the inquisitive element dominates the human mind, which continues to make discoveries. Without scientific discoveries and innovations, no progress can be made in any field. And the moot point is that to think and inquire through our intellect is fundamental to the rational and discerning mind the humans possess. Centuries ago, Galileo said, "I do not feel obliged to believe that the same God who has endowed us with sense, reason, and intellect has intended us to forgo their use."[62]

The mind, primarily a rational construct, remains active

throughout life. Highly developed inquisitive rationality is the uniqueness of the human mind.

ii. Part II

Rational Mind and The Brain

As mentioned earlier, the rational mind has a close tie with our brain. Therefore, a short discussion on the human brain may be relevant at this point. The brain is a closely-knit matrix of neurons, synapses, and nerve endings. Anthony Smith, in his book, *The Mind*, has mentioned, "There are 15 billion nerve cells [in human brain], which is also the numeric total (more or less) of stars in our galaxy . . . synapses a thousand-fold greater, and therefore as plentiful as the stars of a thousand galaxies." He also mentions, "The figures of possible connections within our modern brain is as good as infinite."[63] An elephant's brain or that of a whale might be many times bigger and heavier, but none have the complexity of a human brain. The internal complexity of the human brain is so intricate that it is little understood despite science having made significant strides in anatomy and physiology as well as psychiatry and psychology fields. And though links and areas of the brain have been quite well mapped, "but the silent zone is least explored. Within there lies most of mankind's wisdom, imagination, forethought, compassion, and very distinctive lust for life, art, thought invention and despair."[64]

Memory and its Recall

Some may consider the brain as infinite but in fact, it is finite. All areas of brain are interconnected, though there are specific parts for specific functions. There are specific parts for memory retention and recall. However, no part can claim exclusivity regarding memory. An essential ingredient of mind is memory. Memory is the staff around which ideas and feelings are woven. Without memory, perhaps a productive life may just not be possible. Moreover, the faculty of memory is not only corporeal but also cellular. Nevertheless, memory is a boon as well as a baneful contribution. Boon because without memory, things like scientific discoveries and human progress will not be possible. Baneful because there is no mechanism by which one can choose what memory to keep and which ones to discard. Everyone would like to preserve sweet memories, memories of achievements, memorable events, etc., and discard painful memories from the mind but it is not possible. This can be compared to a rose which carries fragrance as well as thorns. So basically, one cannot cherry-pick or erase memory monads, voluntarily. Furthermore, every memory has weightage quality. In other words, every perceptive cue liable to be stored in the memory vault has a strength of penetration in order to embed on the memory plate. Obviously, the ones having higher embedding force will impact deeper and last longer in the memory vault than the ones having a lesser force. It is well-known that most images aggregate in the hippocampus, but it is the amygdala above the hippocampus in human brain that is said to apply a filtering mechanism by which the mind retains or discards an image. Some imageries make a lasting impression and are retained in the mind while some are discarded instantaneously. Memory impressions are like a rubber stamp; if you apply little pressure and just touch it on a paper, it will leave a faint impression, but if you press it hard, the impression will be deeper. That is to say that some memories, like childhood memories of death, sexual abuse etc., may impact the mind (conscious awareness) with greater force than the others, and exhibit as a psychological aberration, later in life.

We have discussed that the hippocampus is the main functioning unit for memory, but even the cerebellum has an important role in the learning of procedural memory. Amygdala, located above the hippocampus, is also known to be associated with emotional learning and memory. Different centres in our brain are so intricately interconnected that function of memory encoding and its retention cannot allude to a single part. Memory recall may be volitional or involuntary. It is volitional when a student recalls mathematical formulae or when one indulges in a repetitive task or an act. It is involuntary when a memory sprouts from the subconscious on its own. Also, the force of the impact on conscious awareness will be proportional to the qualitative strength of the recalled or appeared memory. Every recalled memory monad strikes on the plate of the superego and creates vibrations. These vibrations may just pass off or cause a certain type of feeling which may range from anguish to joy.

Perception and Memory Recall

Let us once again recapitulate the possible flow of sense perception and activation of action organs. Once a perception is captured, it is transmitted to the brain (corporeal element), and from there, it travels to the mind (an abstract element). The brain compares all this data with previous records already stored and identifies the sensory cue. Therefore, all the stimuli collected through touch, smell, sight, hearing, etc., get analysed, and stored as memory in the different parts of the brain, the hippocampus being the principal repository. However, it is through the recall and comparison that the mind can determine in a jiffy between an apple and a lemon. The intuitive and instinctive recall is instantaneous.

It is pertinent to mention that perception gathered by senses have their distinct qualia. Take the touch sensation for example. The recipient of touch is generally able to feel the differences between a warm and a lukewarm handshake. Individuals, especially females, can easily differentiate between a friendly, fatherly, and sensual touch. Each type of sensation does not need to be perceived only through earlier experiences in the extant life. How does a woman distinguish between a fatherly and sensual touch? Sensory impulse is the same but somewhere in the unconscious she relates the quality of touch and identifies a sensual touch or a fatherly touch. All such sensations are already ingrained in mind somewhere, most likely in the collective unconscious. No doubt, identification of some sense perceptions come directly from past experiences, but many come from the collective unconscious, a term coined by Carl Jung. Jung hypothesised that past collective experiences in a species are retained in the unconscious in the form of imagery or archetypes, and the entire species unconsciously and unknowingly act through this attribute of collective unconscious. To illustrate this further, I must recount an empirical observation from my personal experience.

I stay in a multi-storeyed residential society. Normally we see pigeons frolicking the whole day. One day, I found they had just disappeared. I was contemplating on the cause when I saw a falcon perched upon a pipe projection. So, that was the reason, I concluded. After a few minutes, due to nothing to prey upon, the predator flew off and the pigeons returned in hordes. This is an example of how collective unconscious works. It was not that each pigeon had experienced the imminent danger in their present life but knew to safeguard from the predatory bird and returned to their usual activity only after the threat left. They were able to feel the imminent danger through their collective unconscious.

The collective unconscious is the means through which our mind cognises a situation, carries out a comparative study, and triggers an action. It takes a deep dive into the vast library stored in the unconscious mind that lets us compare an input. This comparison and identification in the mental faculty are instantaneous. The top speed of neuro-somatic impulse transmission is about one hundred meters per second. In other words, a direction by the brain to the intended organ, such as the toes, will travel at this speed when one wants to bend his toes. This is awfully slow compared to computing speed. Electricity, which powers a computer, travels almost at the speed of light, which is 186,000 miles (300,000 km) per second.[65] Also, the travelling time of an impulse for a bodily action requires a fraction of a second. However, the cognition, comparison, construction of opinion, and conclusion in the example given above is instantaneous. Therefore, it is quite evident that thoughts travel at a much faster pace than neural impulses and are not dependent upon neural transmission. Many more examples can be quoted to understand that an instant reaction is not the handiwork of the brain but of mind. It substantiates the view that computation in mind takes place at lightning speed. In the contemplation of Baruch Spinoza, "We all have flashes of perfect knowledge, and therefore have glimpses of what *'scientia intuitiva'* would be."[66] That is how we can distinguish between an apple and a guava instantaneously. Also, the sixth-sense experience and intuitive thoughts are such facultative outcome. Against this, solving a mathematical problem is not instantaneous. It requires recall of stacked memory from personal life. For example, a child appearing in an examination will have to recall his didactic learning before answering a question. He cannot solve a problem instantaneously. The delay in such cases is due to the computing brain coming in the process of task completion.

iii. Part III

Personal and Collective Unconscious

Freud and Jung, famous psychiatrists and psychoanalysts, considered two states of mind—the conscious and the unconscious. Freud initially labelled the unseen part of the mind as subconscious but later called it unconscious. Jung also discarded the term subconscious in the favour of unconscious but differed from Freud on the explanation. Personal experience is different from the collective instinct, and therefore Jung agreed, and perhaps at the same time differed to an extent with the Freudian concept of the unconscious. Freud believed that the unconscious was a product of personal experiences, whereas Jung posited that it was the product of collective experiences inherited through the genes.[67] After all, genes are repository as well as experience recorder. He maintained that there were two types of collective unconscious: the personal unconscious and the collective unconscious. If one looks critically at the Freudian and Jungian literature, it appears that personal and collective unconscious differ widely in their concept, nature, and acquisition. Personal unconscious is individualistic whereas collective unconscious is the innate collective tendency in all the members of a species as a whole. Jung, in his lecture at St Bartholomew's Hospital at London, delivered on October 19, 1936, said: "My thesis then is as follows: in addition to our immediate consciousness, which is of a thoroughly personal nature . . . , there exists a second psychic system of a collective, universal, and impersonal nature which is identical in all individuals. This collective unconscious does not develop individually but is inherited . . ."[68] He also said, "A more or less superficial layer of unconscious is undoubtedly personal. I call it personal unconscious. But this personal unconscious rests upon a deeper layer, which . . . is inborn . . . I call the collective unconscious."[69] Therefore, it is apparent that there is a remarkable difference between personal unconscious and collective unconscious. Freud and Jung stated that there are only two states—conscious and unconscious and did not use the term subconscious. For them, what was not in the conscious was in the unconscious. But such demarcation raises some issues. As we understand, the term personal unconscious relates to forgotten experiences, facts, happenings, and repressed emotional contents in a person's present life. It may relate to simple matters, like forgetting someone's name or a chemical equation your teacher taught you in your school, or utterly grave experiences of a heinous crime you may have committed, an experience of abuse in the childhood, or sexual exploitation later in life. All such experiences are not lost but dip as personal unconscious in the subconscious mind, eventually reflecting in a person's behaviour. You can try to rake up your brain to recover the lost data and regain the forgotten memory, or it may sprout up on its own affecting the future behaviour pattern. Practicing psychiatrists come across plentiful of such cases. A female sexually abused in her childhood may develop a hateful attitude towards the male gender, in general. Similarly, a male child sexually abused, or exploited may develop hatred towards others, or turn antisocial. These horrific experiences remain embedded in the psyche (as personal unconscious) and exhibit in the quirky behaviour. Whatever we experience in day-to-day life is what we confront in the conscious state. However, all that we experience, learn, or witness does not remain in the conscious focus all the time else our cognitive canvas will get all jumbled up. Therefore, all these recede into the background, and the background, in this case, is the subconscious for easy recovery (volitional or involuntary) and not the unconscious where instincts reign, not rationality.

Thus, we find that there are two classes of experiences. One from the extant life, and the other the experiential outcome and impressions we carry from past lives. In Jungian contemplation, these two are different but contained in the same vault, that is unconscious. But the fact remains that these two—the feelings, emotions, experiences accumulating from our present life and the imageries, experiences, or archetypes carried from the previous lives—are two different entities. Going by the Jungian classification both would appear to be contained in the same, that is the unconscious, which appears a little confusing. That is why the later generation philosophers and New Age literature suggest the terminology of 'subconscious', and now it is mostly agreed that subconscious and unconscious though similar, bear slightly different connotation. The subconscious and unconscious are notebook pages where the mind preserves the sticky notes. However, it is pertinent to note that collective unconscious is forceful, uncovering many unexplained aspects of life, not usually apparent. The past is never extirpated, its vestige occupies a place in your mind like fallen dry leaves squeaking under your feet to make its presence felt. To quote from a poem of T. S. Eliot:

"I have said before
That the past experience revived in the meaning
Is not the experience of one life only
But of many generations—not forgetting
Something that is probably quite ineffable:"
— 'The Dry Salvages', T. S. Eliot

Three Dimensions of Mind

The mind is the most complex and enigmatic organ in living species. Hence, it is not easy to understand the mind. It is a daunting task for any philosopher, scientist, or thinker to understand and describe the human mind in its totality. However, the effort must go on! We are trying to decipher the hieroglyphs of mind to know the functioning of mind-brain or mind-body relationship. As mentioned above, the mind is discussed here in three layers and three substrates in an effort to simplify its complexity. The three layers are rational, instinctive, and intuitive, and the three substrates are conscious, subconscious, and unconscious, the conscious being most apparent, the subconscious a little deeper, and the unconscious even deeper. The mind rests within these layers and substrates. So, let us try to understand what these are. But before that, and first and foremost, it is important to know that these are not strictly compartmentalised; all these layers and substrates are interconnected and work in close coordination and conjunction. It would be a folly to consider these explicitly separate and different. I have considered the mind into these layers and substrates (based on its functionality) only for an easy understanding.

a) Layer1: The Rational Mind

We all use the rational mind in our day-to-day affairs to help us decide our course of action. The rational mind is objective and it interacts with the external objects, receives inputs from the sense organs, acts accordingly, and sets up a feeling or imagery. The mind undertakes a comparative study with the in-built feelings, emotions, and imageries to identify an object perception. Once perceptive input is analysed, a decision is arrived at whether the required response will be somatic or otherwise. If it is somatic, the relevant centres in the brain activate action organs and if not, a feeling or imagery is formed and stored in the vault of the subconscious. The interrelatedness of the rational mind and brain is well established. Any physical or physiological damage to the brain may limit or modify facultative mental activity, and similarly, any psychiatric anomaly (mental aberration) may affect the brain resulting in an altered behaviour. In both these cases, one may exhibit behavioural anomalies and abnormalities, but in the former, the cause lies outside the physical brain and in the latter, the cause lies in the brain itself, affecting rational thinking and rational behaviour. Therefore, persons with such disabilities are devoid of rationality.

Societal Norms and Rational Behaviour

Rational feeling and behaviour are the expected and accepted outcome of object perception. This 'accepted outcome' would be the known 'normal' when it meets the parameters laid down by society based on its social values, or own superconscious-the untiring watch over your mind. In other words, the behaviour that conforms to the social norms and parameters will be termed as normal. Parameters of societal norms are not the handiwork of one generation but collective social and cultural outcome over decades and centuries. Each generation necessarily undergoes material changes in its outlook and lay fresh social norms over current practices. What we know as societal norms are the current parameters. Each of us thinks seriously about how will 'I will be looked upon' by society and try to modify or modulate our behaviour accordingly to fit within the parameters. Rational thinking is the ability to consider available inputs, relevance, and variables of a situation to arrive at a sound decision (see Fig 3).

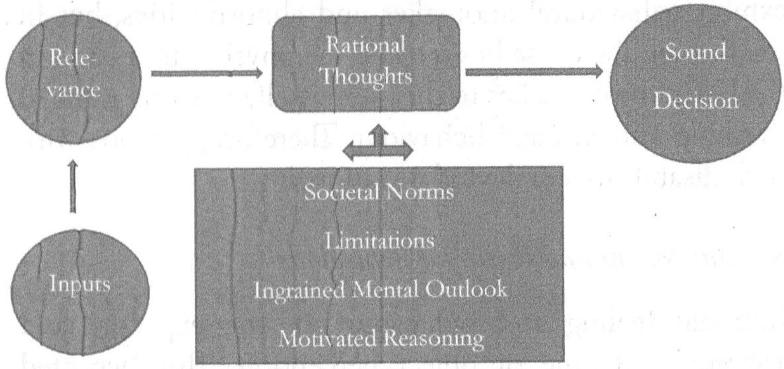

Figure 3: Input to Decision Process

Here you can see that relevance of a sensory input is determined with rationality, which is influenced by societal norms, limitations, acted upon by the ingrained individualised mental outlook, and reasoning (including motivated reasoning). In other words, society influences individual behaviour. Since individuals are the bricks of society, individually and collectively, they contribute to the development of social norms. So, the social influence on the individual and the individual influence on society are complementary to each other. Every society has its own social norms, and so the individual behaviour will be different in different societies. Social norms of Western societies will not be the same as the relatively conservative Indian society. How 'we meet and greet' will be different in different societies as well as in different religious groups and countries. Individual behaviour within a family, extended family, and society will be different as the social values and expectations will be somewhat different. Take, for example, a successful politician. His behaviour will be different within his family compared to his behaviour with the people he works with, his political circle, and society he serves. However, it is worth noting that an accepted universal definition in this regard as to what is 'normal' might not be possible because the social order keeps changing. With each generation, newer norms and values modify the already existent norms. A few decades ago (at least in India), even a thought of divorce would raise eyebrows and live-in relationships were not common. But now, no one really bothers much about divorce and live-in relations. Therefore, the rational response will be different than what may have been decades ago.

Irrational Thinking and Behaviour

So basically, rational thinking is the ability to consider available inputs, relevance, and variables of a situation to arrive at a sound decision. That is why when we conclude some cogent argument, it is said to be 'well thought out'. Poor decisions and mistakes are the results of flawed thinking, which may be due to wrong or faulty cognition and interpretation of inputs, influenced by self-held beliefs or motivated reasoning. Motivated reasoning comes in when one is predisposed to an idea, considers it justified, and tries to find reasons in a hindsight. However, a sound decision presupposes the use of pure reasoning and not motivated reasoning. Yet, the parameters of rationality in a thinking process are not static. They keep changing with changes in social norms and time. When a thought converts to an act, it migrates to the arena of behaviour which may be rational or irrational depending upon whether it was a result of rational or irrational thinking. For example, thinking to swim in a shark-infested sea would be termed irrational, and when some foolhardy converts this to a real act, it will be labelled as irrational behaviour.

Sense of Association

Many times, in the conscious stage (awaken state), a thought generates but escapes immediate capture. We try to recapture but are not able to do so instantaneously. Then we make conscious efforts through our rational mind to capture imageries immediately preceding the lost thought, idea, or image but do not succeed every time. Then we try to recapitulate thoughts that passed through our mind just before the lost thought, and at times, successfully recapitulate. This phenomenon is known as the 'sense of association.' The phenomenon of sense of association is a part of rational thinking and includes revisiting events in time and place, the associating features of the object idea, comparative memory, etc. By comparative memory, I mean the faculty of comparison, which is an innate quality of our mind and it is always active. Our mind goes into comparison mode to determine the quality of an object that comes in the mental focus through sense organs, memory, or past impressions. Data from all our experiences, whether educational, empirical, material, or immaterial, are stored in the subconscious. The mental computer searches from its storehouse all similar and dissimilar imageries, ideas, and feelings with the instrument of objective rationality and then analyses it to conclude the identity of the object.

Let me give an example. You meet someone in a party or a marriage gathering, and someone introduces a person as Mr A as a distant relative. Then someone explains the relationship. It forms an impression or an associating idea in your mind. Later, you try but are unable to recollect the relationship. It is because that imagery has sunk into your subconscious. Then you start raking your mind, trying to recapitulate. If the connection comes to the fore then well and good, but if it does not then you start searching for associating cues. You try and recapitulate who introduced the person and then identify the foggy identity through the process of association. The association of ideas or impressions is a critical attitude of the mind. Similarly, you may discover the connecting bond through the recapitulation of stored imageries and ideas in the subconscious. If that does not work, the mind tries to get the supporting data from the superconscious. The superconscious is supposedly infinite as the cosmic consciousness. However, to connect with the superconscious is not usual. One can reach the superconscious with forceful thoughts and concentration. For that, the mind must be conditioned through meditative concentration. It is like connecting a computer with the Bluetooth or wi-fi to the supercomputer, and this takes focusing the mind through concentration and *sadhana*. It does not come easily.

Logic and reasoning are the two most important features of a rational mind. The mind-brain connection remains an enigma, but the rational mind has a closer and more intimate working relationship with the cognitive brain than instinctive or intuitive minds. As against lower species, a rational human mind is capable of inventing new ideas, make scientific discoveries, and explore and deliberate on metaphysical concepts.

b) Layer 2: The Instinctive Mind

As the heading suggests, the instinctive mind is the part of the mind that works on instincts. Instincts are mental attributes that the human mind has carried through the evolutionary process which encompasses experiences of its predecessors. All these experiences are not lost forever but show in subsequently evolved species in one form or the other. The human mind, in its evolution, carried many features of the mind of previous species—these bundle-in to what we call instinct. Differences in instinctual behaviour in different species aren't entirely the same or distinct but seem to overlap. For example, the will to survive is the most basic instinct in all living species and though instinctive actions to survive among humans and animals may be different, the primary aim to survive remains the same. With this aim, a living body also develops an innate sense of safeguards (instinctive actions) which surface in the form of reactive behaviour to a dangerous stimulus specific to a species. And more developed the species, more are the ways to safeguard. You touch a snail crawling and it immediately envelops its body in its shell. It does not try to run away . . . that is its instinct. So, there is a hardwired connection somewhere in its mind-brain complex that triggers such instinctive behaviour. The snail dips in the storehouse of the collective unconscious that guides it to take precautionary measures to draw its body inside the protection of its shell. Similarly, a child quickly withdraws his fingers from a flame which is an instinctive reaction. Some may consider it as a reflex action, but there is a thin line separating instinctive and reflex actions. In both, the neural path could be the same, that is without the involvement of the consciously aware brain. Such reactions are rendered primarily by instincts.

A behaviour is considered instinctive if it is performed without bearing on previous experience of extant life. Newly hatched sea turtles on a beach instinctively move toward the ocean. On birth, marsupials climb into the mother's pouch instinctively. Mind you that they do not have any experience from the present life as they have just been born. Thus, we can see that instincts are innate and have specific intricate patterns of behaviour existing in all the members of a species. It is collective and specific to a species. If one snail withdraws its body in its shell, all will. The instinctive behaviour of a flock of pigeons to fly away, disappear, and hide on sighting a prey bird is an innate instinctive behaviour of the entire species.

Instincts are an innate tendency of a living species to perform an action unconsciously and instinctively. It correlates with the collective unconscious. Instincts remain in-depth and do not stand out perpetually in the realm of our conscious awareness. Philosophers call it a concept of innatism, a doctrine that holds that mind is born with knowledge which a living species uses unconsciously and instinctively. The doctrine of innatism was postulated by the Greek philosopher, Pluto, and later by Descartes. Carl Jung believed that the human mind retained fundamental, unconscious and the biological aspects of our ancestors—the primordial images.[70] Such postulates approximate closely with the Hindu philosophy of transmigration of the soul (metempsychosis), where a soul supposedly carries experiences and impressions to the next embodiment.

Against this, John Locke (1632-1704), an English philosopher and empiricist, advocated that whatever one gains towards building a tendency is based on experiences in one's life and is not carried from previous lives.[71] The point to note here is that both these differing thoughts commonly supported the postulate that experiences build instinctive tendencies in individuals. But most philosophers and metaphysicists agree to the doctrine of innatism that explains instinctive behaviour.

c) Layer 3: The Intuitive Mind

Intuition is to capture factual knowledge without recourse to conscious reasoning. Christmas Humphreys (1901-1983), founder the Buddhist Society in London in 1924, said, "Beyond the intellect, which is the machinery of thought, is the plane of intuition, the faculty of immediate, direct cognition of reality."[72] Intuitive outcome bypasses rationality and logic. It cannot be explained by studying the brain circuitry. Therefore, one may assume that intuition is illogical. That sounds all right seen from the viewpoint of rationality and purely in mathematical parlance. However, in the overall consideration of mental functions, this may not be a valid assessment. Intuitive decisions are also known as gut feelings, which play a decisive role in our lives.

Ancient philosophers from world over have deliberated on intuition and though there have been varying explanations, the accepted commonality is that intuition is some feeling that comes out of the unconscious, i.e., cognised unconsciously. When we cognise an object consciously, we are well aware of the object. Sense organs capture the properties of the object and its analysis and comparison take place in the conscious rational mind. Whereas in the faculty of intuition, the genesis is not cognised through sense organs but with an intuitive mind where usual conscious cues and steps of cognition are transcended. Radhakrishnan (1888-1975), an Indian philosopher who later became president of India, says, "There is something transcending the consciousness of self to which many names are given—intuition, revelation, cosmic consciousness, and God vision . . . so we call it super-consciousness."[73]

It is believed that over time, intuitive power declined in the human mind with physiological and psychological development, just like the decline of instinctual ability. Ants, rats, and birds can anticipate natural disasters before the human mind can. However, intuitive features can be reinforced through meditation and some yogic exercises. Some ascetics claim to have developed the intuitive faculty of clairvoyance and clairaudience. Sri Aurobindo (1872-1950), an Indian philosopher, believed that intuitive knowledge was common in ancient Vedic people, which was overshadowed by science of reason. Osho believed in a gradual transformation of consciousness in human beings from animal instinct to intelligence and then to intuition. "Like instinct, at the other polarity of your being, beyond the mind which is the world of intellect, is the world of intuition."[74] Buddhism places intuition beyond the mental process of conscious thinking. In Islam, intuition has been considered as mystical and prophetic. Pluto considered intuition as the pre-existing knowledge residing in the soul of eternity and a phenomenon by which one becomes conscious of pre-existing knowledge.[75] Sigmund Freud considered that knowledge could be gained only by observation and rejected by other means, including intuition. Carl Jung defined intuition as perception via the unconscious.[76] Thus, we can see that the faculty of intuition has drawn much debate and deliberation since ancient times. Many ignore the intuitive spark evaluating it on the plank of rationality. Then the spark peters out and is no more actionable. The rationality in you pours a bucket of water extinguishing the intuitive spark.

a) Substrate 1: The Conscious Mind

Conscious Awareness

In simple terms, conscious awareness is being aware of the self and surroundings. This may be a simplistic explanation of a complex subject but many philosophers and thinkers have pondered over the phenomenon of consciousness and awareness. Many approximated consciousness with the brain, and since awareness is through the brain, many proposed that consciousness may be just an abstruse extension of awareness. However, we know that consciousness continues to work even if the brain is not fully functional. Therefore, consciousness has to be different than awareness. Also, if consciousness is the same as awareness, then the conscious mind and awakened state should be the same, which is not true. Thus, we can conclude that consciousness is an abstract quale of mind and is different from awareness which is a gross state of a living object. Another aspect is that consciousness is only one of the qualia of mind and does not depict the mind in its wholeness. Reducing the mind to only the state of consciousness is incorrect as we also have the subconscious and unconscious parts. Therefore, it is apparent that consciousness is only one of the states of mind. Moreover, the state of consciousness is the priori to awareness which has gradations. A person fully aware of the surrounding may be at a higher state of awareness, whereas a doping person may have little awareness of his surroundings. Such a person is at a lower level of awareness and behaves without complete conscious awareness. As mentioned earlier, man is a social animal. His conscious outreach is with the external objects. A complete awareness is being aware of the interrelatedness and interconnections with others, the surroundings, and with the universe. It is not enough to appreciate the physical presence of nature but what are its wants and needs. It is not only being aware of another person but being aware of all the emotional and qualitative attributes of another person. It is not only knowing your own emotions and feelings but of others as well. A self-centric person will be highly aware of his or her emotions and feelings but not of others. Take for example, two friends A and B. A not only is aware of himself but also knows the surroundings qualitatively. As against this B knows his own awareness but not of the surroundings. Therefore, B will be at a lower level of awareness. He remains self-absorbed and has little regard for the outside. Construed to individual relatedness, B will not be bothered how the other person would feel. Such people act and react in an impulsive and instinctual manner as animals do. As against this, a person who is egalitarian by nature, and spiritually inclined will be at a higher level of conscious awareness.

Sense Perception and Conscious Awareness

Consciousness is being aware of perception gathered from what is presented to the senses. Sensory energy inputs are conveyed through the neural system to the concerned centre in our brain and to the mind and then compared and analysed through rationality. Conception follows a well-known process: object perception—impression—comparison—analysis—imagination—action or effectual outcome. But firstly, the mind has to acknowledge the input; then only it will start the process of analysis. The analysis is influenced by many factors, as depicted in Figure 4.

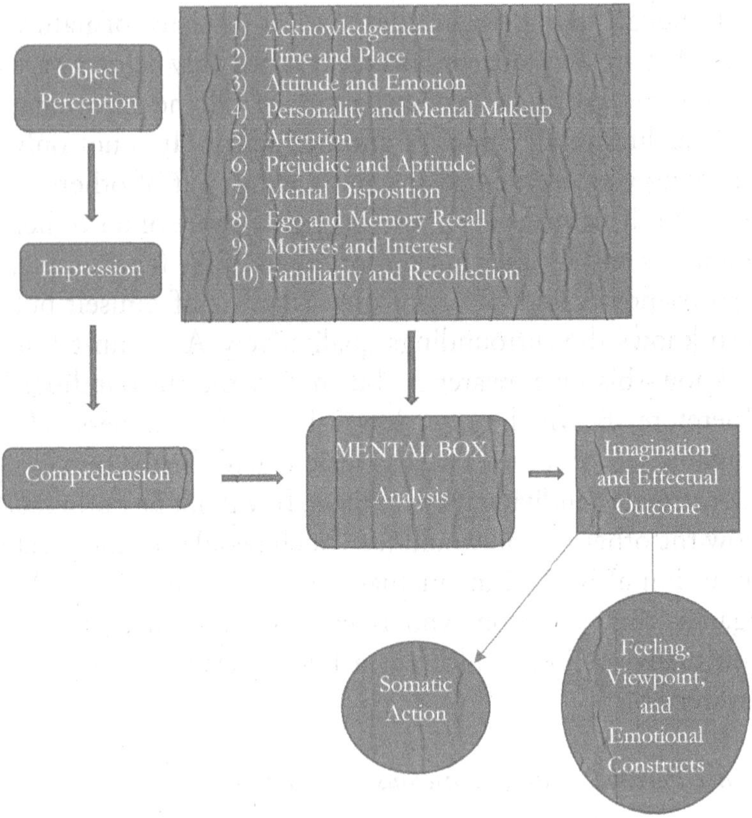

Figure 4: Sense Perception to Effectual Outcome

Once the process of analysis is complete, the effectual outcome is either a somatic action or mental construct of a feeling, a viewpoint, or an emotional build-up. David Hume (1711-1776 AD) while deliberating on the issue says ". . . since nothing is ever present to the mind but perceptions, and since all ideas are derived from something antecedently present to the mind; . . . it is impossible for us . . . to conceive or form an idea of anything specifically different from ideas and impressions."[77]

Therefore, in the process of conception, it may be reiterated that nothing can be conceived without the intervention of the mind. And since every human mind is unique and plastic, the conception will differ in accordance with time and space as described earlier. It would, therefore, follow that being conscious is not only being aware of the surroundings but also being aware that your mind is consciously aware. You must have experienced during a walk in a park that you missed to take notice of some objects your friend or your spouse cognised. It is not that the visual cue was not there, but your mind missed it. If the mind is immersed in another deep thought, it may miss noticing objects and fail to acknowledge visual or auditory cues. Cognition of an object, therefore, is an extension of your mind, as explained earlier. In other words, the external object is an extension of your internal mental faculty, akin to what saints and seers say that the material world is an extension of universal consciousness.

Thus, we have the sense organs for perception, the analytic mind to analyse, and the brain for bodily action. But this is limited to the ability of the brain a person possesses. When you want to concentrate on an issue, it is necessary to focus on the issue at hand. Sense perception interacts with the rational brain leading to a subjective feeling (that is as perceived by your mind). It creates a thought-vibration, and thus your mind may get distracted. But when we close the conduit of other conscious experiences, our mind concentrates on the issue. That is why it is said that conscious awareness can be liberated to a much higher plane "when freed up from the shackles of the physical brain,"[78] the basis of meditation. However, it is not correct to assume that meditation can be practised with closed eyes only. Many are known to have achieved meditation while engaged in usual activities. Shri Ramakrishna Paramhansa (1836-1886), the mystic Indian, is said to enter into *samadhi* and assume meditating posture while talking or walking. But it may not be for all to achieve such capability; it may be obtainable with prolonged *Sadhana.*

Levels of Awareness

Awareness (integral to conscious mind), can be stratified mainly in three stages, the woken state, the sleep state, and the deep sleep state. In the sleep state, one can recall dreams, whereas, in the deep sleep state, one may not experience dreams, a dreamless sleep. All must have experienced while going to sleep one first goes into a sleeping mode, then enters the state of deep sleep. In the process of awakening, one undergoes the same steps in the reverse. When you close the lid of the laptop, it goes to sleep, but when you shut down the computer, it goes to slumber and takes longer to reawaken. All must have experienced short duration dreams while waking from deep sleep to sleep, and just before awaking. The mind, therefore, undergoes stages in regaining woken awareness. Apart from these three states of awareness, there is another state called the *Turiya* state which is the fourth state. *Turiya* is a state of awareness that transcends all other states.

Experience is consciousness plus the object. If there is no object then there will be no experience, and similarly, if there is no consciousness there will be no experience. It is important to understand that awareness is not the same as consciousness. Consciousness is a deeper attribute, even more subtle than the mind. When your *Turiya* state is awakened you see the seeing, you experience the experiencing. When you observe an object with your gross sense organ, it is seen with your gross brain and then with the subtle mind, and finally, with the inner self (*Turiya* state). All experiences are evaluated by the fourth state—the *Turiya* state.

Swami Sarvpriyananda of Ramakrishna Math Order relates an interesting mythical parable in the lecture to IIT Kharagpur on April 30, 2014[79]:

> The great king Janaka (7th century BCE) of Mithila kingdom had an interest in philosophy and many prominent sages of the time, including Ashtavakra, visited his court regularly for philosophical discussions. On one particular night, he went to sleep as usual but was awakened in the middle of a night by his guards who informed him about an enemy attack on his kingdom. All stirred up by this unexpected event, he quickly got up, wore his armour, gathered his army, and went to battle, but to no avail. He and his army were defeated and he was brought down to a level of a beggar and was exiled from his kingdom. King Janaka then suddenly woke from his dream, all sweating and panting. He realised that all that had happened was only a dream, even though it felt real. The next morning, he presided over his daily court but the dream from the previous night kept tormenting him. All he could do was repeat the phrase, "*Woh sach hai ya yeh sach hai*? (Was that the truth or is this the truth?)" He was gripped by this doubt and kept on repeating the phrase. Everyone in his court was perturbed by

this ordeal and no matter who approached him, he kept on saying, "*Woh sach hai ya yeh sach hai?*" Then the wise sage Ashtavakra came to the court. He approached the king and asked him, "Were you present in the battle that you lost?" King Janaka answered, "Yes, I was present there." The sage then questioned him, "And are you present here?" The king replied, "Yes, I am present here." "So, you are saying that you are here and were there as well?" the sage queried. The king answered, "Yes," and then repeated the same phrase, "*Par woh sach hai ya yeh sach hai?*" After contemplating for a short while, the sage expounded, "Neither that was the truth nor this is the truth." What the sage meant was that everything we experience in the dream state as well as in the waking state is false; the only truth is the self—the true reality. This state of self-realisation is known as *Turiya*. It is the background that pervades and underlies all states of consciousness.

Moksha in the State of Awareness

Moksha is also a state of awareness. *Nyaya* and *Vaisesika* schools teach that *Moksha* can be experienced only after death, whereas Samkhya and Vedanta teach that it can be attained during a living state as well. Attaining the state of *Moksha* in the Vedanta philosophy is when one develops complete control over his senses; conquers individual ego, anger, avarice, desire, sorrow, and grief etc., and remains unaffected even under great provocation. Such a person would be said to have attained *Moksha* in life itself. It is also said that complete *Moksha* can be obtained only when *the Vasanas* or the desire of all types are annihilated which takes place only in *Nirvikalpa Samadhi. Nirvikalpa* Samadhi is a form of deep meditation without focusing on an object where thoughts are said to cease. You enter a state of 'no mind', a state where the usual activities of the mind are stilled. This simply means you let go of your perceptive awareness, set it aside. The mind meditates without an object, not even on the Almighty in the focus. It is said to bring infinite bliss and peace and is difficult to describe even by those who have experienced it as it is a state beyond human mind and thinking. It would be plain and simple for any person to understand that such meditating practice may not be possible for a householder, and therefore not practical. But trying to achieve such a state would always be possible.

One can realise *Moksha* in the earlier stage of life, not necessarily at the fag-end. Many have renounced the world early in life and engaged in penance and meditation in the higher reaches of the Himalayas. The Buddha also renounced the material world in the early part of his life and attained a state of *Moksha*. Adi Shankara and Swami Vivekananda are examples from the recent past; many may have been in the ancient world. *Moksha* is, after all, a state of self-realised awareness. It can be attained at any stage in life. *Moksha* after death is for the soul, not for the body-soul complex, or mind-body complex. It may be a permanent state where the soul is freed from birth, death, and rebirth, whereas the state of *Moksha* attained in extant life may be transient. It lasts till one consciously remains master of his senses and his mind. It lasts till one remains detached in the higher state of awareness. Attaining a state of detachment in life is more complicated but fruitful than working for whole life towards attaining *Moksha* after death. Realising *Moksha* in life is the attaining a higher platform because one realises the true self in one's own life. It may sound easy, but it is the most difficult to achieve. That is why it is not for everyone to attain a state of *Moksha* in one's life.

Altered States of Awareness

We have discussed different states of awareness, and how can one change the state of awareness under normal circumstances by meditation etc. But there is another way to change the conscious awareness, that is by artificial means. There are natural and chemical compounds known and used to alter the state of consciousness and awareness. I will be using three terms, the altered state of consciousness, altered awareness, and altered behaviour. State of consciousness is a mental state, whereas altered state of awareness is the varied results of the mental state, and altered behaviour is the exhibited part of altered awareness. So, when one uses a psychedelic or psychoactive substance, first the state of consciousness changes. This gives rise to changed awareness where the person views the same surroundings, the same objects differently. It results in a changed behaviour which is the exhibited part. Hypothetically, if we bundle all different states of awareness exhibited in a person's behaviour in the cross-section of a population, we can arrive at an average value. In other words, a state of consciousness and exhibited awareness and behaviour that is acceptable to society as the norm. Any variation can be labelled as altered behaviour. One can attain altered state of consciousness through meditation, yoga, mystic rituals, and mystic dance etc., and also with psychoactive and psychedelic substances and drugs. Human beings have never been satisfied with what nature has provided and always try to find better (as assumed) different planes of consciousness. As the 'grass is greener on the other side' one feels something exotic lies on the side of altered state of consciousness! Life is experiential but also experimental. One always tries to experiment. Therefore, for some getting hooked on to psychedelic or psychoactive substances is just a life-experiment.

Plants with medicinal value have been used to alter the state of consciousness since ancient times. The earliest evidence of the use of psychoactive substances dates back to even ten thousand years, and historical evidence of cultural use over the past five thousand years[80]. Based on archaeological evidence researchers have concluded that the practice of chewing of coco leaves dates back to over eight thousand years ago in Peruvian society[81]. Humans have experimented with many other methods to alter the state of consciousness apart from the use of plant and fruit derivatives. For example, the whirling dance of the dervish, rituals in the form of ecstatic dances in India, and many other societies to attain religious ecstasy are some examples. Witchcraft, Gypsy dance, etc., are mostly practised to achieve altered consciousness. The performer goes into a trans and reaches altered awareness, supposedly for an ethereal experience. All such activities are aimed to derive spiritual experience to realise the divine. How much it helps to realise the divine is anybody's guess. Moreover, use or misuse of psychoactive plant or psychedelic chemical derivatives appears to have afflicted human society of the day, rather adversely. All these are either habit-forming, addictive, or cause dependence.

"Mohan Singh (fictitious name) was one of the employees in my ancestral household. He was from a reasonably decent farmer family. He was hooked on to smoking ganja (marijuana). We, the children, used to play around near him most of the time outside our study hours. When I look back, I can still visualise those red-shot eyes, apparently looking at something but actually looking not at any object in the sight. In some respects, he was a miserable man, committed theft when my parents and all of us were away and his services were terminated. Stolen silverware, gold ornaments, and gems were never recovered. Another incident includes one of my classmates in my medical school who was addicted to morphine. Of late, he had been showing behavioural changes apparent in the interaction with others. He used to take the injection daily at about 12 in the afternoon. One day, while we were having tea in the college canteen, I just wondered where he was. A senior looked at me quizzically and remarked, 'You cannot find him at this hour of the day. If you have to find him, go to his room in the hostel. He must be loading a syringe with his honey-love potion. One day, in his room, he was found dead due to an overdose of morphine."

These are just a few examples from my personal life; others may have many more. Use of psychedelic drugs in rave parties to alter the state of consciousness is quite common in the present-day modern societies. It is prevalent across all socio-economic sections, not necessarily limited to night club frequenting affluent class. There appears a direct connection between the fast life of the present-day world and the use (more appropriately, misuse) of psychedelic and psychoactive drugs. However, psychoactive substances have medicinal value as well. A host of medicinal preparations are used in different psychic disorders, and for physiological needs, such as keeping awake during exams or for inducing sleep in other circumstances or as pain-relieving agent. It is reported that the brain can be put in a state of suspended animation (absence of woken awareness) by lowering the temperature to about 10 degrees Celsius.[82] It helps the surgeon to carry on with surgery for a prolonged period. Of course, it is pointed out that this is only a news item and not based on peer-reviewed research paper. Therefore, one may not get taken by it.

Environmental Pollution and Behavioural Change

However, the behavioural changes we see in society today are not all due to use or misuse of psychedelic or psychoactive drugs. But are also due to chemical pollution. People are generally more aggressive and 'short on fuse' these days. Road rage is experienced daily in major cities in India. Angry outburst turns to even shooting incidents. Roadside criminal activities are on the rise. Criminality against women has shown a quantum jump in the recent past. All these cannot be attributed only to a stressful fast life, or misuse of drugs but are also due to environmental pollution leading to changed behaviour. This digression is necessary to inform that environmental pollution is another major factor affecting the conscious behaviour adversely. Air, water, vegetables we consume these days are polluted with mercury, lead, arsenic, etc. Lead, and mercury poisoning impacts neural circuit resulting in changed behaviour. The primary source of lead pollution is gasoline. Its main effects are on the central nervous system, the urinary system, and the gastrointestinal systems. Changes in personality, such as increased irritability, convulsions and delirium have been reported due to lead and mercury pollution. Mercury is neurotoxic, causing changes in personality and behaviour, apart from many other debilitating outcomes. It also impacts neural development in a child. In the case of overt cases of lead or mercury poisoning, a person is admitted in hospitals for treatment and management. However, it is the sub-clinical pollution the human body carries that is a matter of concern. They do not need to be hospitalised and are not aware of it. They exhibit altered behaviour as a result of altered state of consciousness.

b) Substrate 2: The Subconscious Mind

Memory Recall through Subconscious

The subconscious mind is the second substrate of the mind-brain relationship. Thoughts can vanish into the subconscious and can also arise from the subconscious. It is the repository of feelings and emotional constructs which influences individual behaviour and inclination. As the name suggests, the subconscious is an underlying labyrinth, a substrate of the human mind where thoughts and feelings reside to come out to conscious awareness as and when required. In other words, the subconscious is generally at the command of the conscious, but not always as certain ideas and imagery may jump into the conscious awareness involuntarily. There are instances when you realise that your Subconscious has acted independently of the conscious. Suppose that you have a prolonged conversation with your friend and discuss many topics. After a few days, you meet again and try to recollect the name of a particular person you had discussed in your previous meeting but fail to recall. You rake up your memory but are unable to recall the name howsoever hard you try. You return home and get into the routine. Suddenly, while washing your dish in the kitchen, the name pops up. You may wonder how is it that the recall took place after a time gap, particularly when you were not thinking about the previous conversation nor trying to recollect the name. The explanation lies in the fact that once a question is raised, and the conscious substrate is unable to provide an immediate answer it gives up. However, the subconscious keeps working on it, and when it grips the answer, it throws it to the conscious substrate.

Subconscious and Emotions

As mentioned before, the subconscious also houses and controls emotions and related human behaviour. The limbic system, especially the amygdala in our brain, is considered associated with emotional processes. Emotions also drive motivation, positive or negative. Extroverts are quite open in expressing their emotions, whereas the introverts are reserved and do not like to share their feelings. Introverts are highly underconfident and feel vulnerable. This class generally is full of pent-up feelings. A person may have emotional outburst on pent-up feelings expressed as anger or despondency. In both these cases, emotion outstrips rationality resulting in impulsive behaviour. A feeling of helplessness seeps in the mind when a person experiences untoward and sad happening in his life where he thinks no effort is likely to get him out, and thus he develops a feeling of despondency. Feeling of sadness cause depression, including suicidal tendencies. Sadness and frustration also may give rise to anger. The reactive outcome may be disproportionate against society or a person depending on the origin of a feeling.

Overall behaviour pattern will largely depend upon

whether a person nurses positive or negative mental vibe towards another. Likes and dislikes are features of emotion and therefore retained in the subconscious mind. Say, for example, you take a liking for a person. The idea of liking gets into the subconscious. The reverse is also true, in the sense that if meet a person and dislike him. In both these cases, there is an emotional build up in the subconscious which modifies one's behaviour towards that particular person. In the same manner, one may develop a predilection towards an idea or a suggestion. In such a case as well, the emotional build-up will be either in favour or against. Emotion engineered ideas and thoughts surface in the conscious which may be supportive to a situation or an issue, or be cynical or outright devilish and diabolical. So, a state of emotion may be joyful, or sad showing in the behaviour. Optimistic people will always have a positive outlook towards the future, and pessimists a negative outlook towards life. Positivism and negativism, therefore, are in the cauldron of emotion giving out vapour of exhibited behaviour, when on the boil. Mind builds a root-template of emotional build-up from where rises a particular emotive thought-essence, influencing behaviour of a person. Emotional behaviour will approximate with the root-template, i.e., constructed emotional build-up in the subconscious. A person who has not done well in life considers three options—to strive hard to catch up, accept his position a result of his fate and destiny, or develop a negative attitude towards his family, society, or the world considering these to be the cause of his failure. Such people are fit candidates to turn out to be anti-social. Emotional constructs do not die out even if the person succeeds later in life. He may retaliate against the supposed cause of the failure (as construed in his mind) when in a position to do so and inflict immense damage to the society or to another person.

The subconscious does not let you forget what you may have undergone in your earlier life. The ember may turn to a full-blown fire. When politicians attain a position of power, they might nurse a revengeful attitude against those who may not have supported him or her in the election. Similarly, an oppressed person turns into a *baghi* (a brigand) later, committing murder and dacoity mainly to take revenge on the people who may have oppressed him or her. One may recall many examples of how a person was tortured or humiliated before turning a brigand or joining a brigand group which roamed the ravines in Chambal, near Gwalior till recently (Such groups have been largely eliminated now with police action or political pro-activism). Thus, it is evident that the repressed feelings come out in the form of criminal and anti-social activities, including emotive outbursts. We find that the subconscious (personal unconscious in Jungian philosophy) stores life experiences, feelings, and imageries influencing individual behaviour and conduct whenever come to the fore.

c) Substrate 3: The Unconscious Mind

The term 'unconscious' also denotes a medical condition when a patient is not aware of the surrounding, and does not respond to external stimuli. However, the discussion here focuses on another in-built feature of the mind, that is the unconscious mind.

Archaic Imageries in the Backyard

We have discussed the conscious and subconscious mind and dilated upon the personal unconscious. Now we will discuss the influence of the experiences of past lives a, retained as what Jung described as the collective unconscious. The third substrate is the unconscious mind. It stores not only images but also archetypes, which are archaic and fossilised imageries, deeply ingrained in one's mind. The unconscious retains repressed feelings, forgotten imageries, and the experiences of past lives as collective unconscious, as against the experiential imageries from present life called the personal unconscious, usually retained in the subconscious mind. Essentially, it consists of the collective experiences of past generations culminating in a collective tendency innate in all members of a species. Jung further argues that "just as organs of the body are not mere lumps of indifferent, passive matter, but are dynamic . . . so also the archetypes as organs of the psyche, are dynamic instinctual complexes . . . The layer of unconscious psyche which is made up of these universal dynamic forms I have termed the collective unconscious."[83] It comes out to the fore on the conscious mind, affecting individual behaviour. Each particular species stores imageries and archaic impressions collectively gathered by cascading generations in the collective unconscious; in other words, the collective unconscious is species-specific. The collective unconscious is much more related to instinctive faculty, unlike the subconscious, which approximates more closely with the intuitive ability. Fleeing flock of doves on sighting a hawk lurking around, or ducks swimming away from gun-toting hunters are examples of instinctive safety actions engineered by the collective unconscious. Whereas recall of an event or a name, etc., in the example quoted in the earlier chapter was closely related to intuitive faculty.

Evolution and Collective Unconscious

The unconscious includes repressed feelings, hidden phobias, concealed perceptions etc. Life of a species, past or present, has been a continuous struggle to survive and evolve. Countless species must have undergone lots of hardship, difficulties, and barriers in the evolutionary history of our living world during the last three to four billion years. Similarly, impressions of hardships faced by our ancestors during the last two to three hundred thousand years of *sapiens* history, and the way these were overcome must have been etched on the memory plate of universal consciousness; and through the universal consciousness in our unconscious mind. Whether one agrees or not with Darwin's theory of evolution, natural selection, or survival of the fittest, no one can deny the struggles living species must have encountered in the successive evolution to *Homo sapiens,* supposedly the most developed species on earth. Evolution is the series of change necessitated by obstruction and contradiction to growth, and memories of such encounters remain collected in the unconscious and come to fore unobtrusively without us being consciously aware of it.

Unconscious the Hidden Workhorse

On the one side, we have tangible cords of human nature that science is continuously discovering; on the other side, we have the vast unexplored ocean of unconscious about which we can only conjecture. The unconscious mind is never at rest; it remains awake during deep sleep, even in a coma state. The unconscious controls many functions of the body, such as cardiovascular, gastrointestinal, respiratory, functions. The difference, however, is that the conscious remains active in a woken state, whereas the unconscious keeps on even when a person is not awake. These two mental levels or mental states-conscious and unconscious work in tandem. The unconscious remains in constant interaction with the conscious, as described by Carl Jung: ". . . Conversely, out of the unconscious, there rises new ideas and tendencies which, as they emerge into consciousness, are known to us as fantasies and impulses. The unconscious is the matrix out of which consciousness grows . . . "[84] With fantasies and impulses, one may like to add 'emotional outburst or emotional outcome' as well, as emotion is an essential aspect of human behaviour. In our contemplation emotions and impulsive behaviour may be from the subconscious, but the overlay could also be from the unconscious.

As said earlier the compartmentalisation of the mind is for easy understanding, these all work in tandem and unison. Impressions on the conscious mind gradually gravitate to the subconscious and the unconscious. Both conscious and unconscious keep blipping thoughts, feelings, forgotten imagery, or memories. However, what springs from the unconscious (from the imageries and archetypes) are strong drivers for unexplained behaviour which are not predisposed.

3
The God Delusion

At the outset, it is necessary to understand that we are not talking about delusion associated with psychiatric conditions, but limiting the discussion to only religious delusion. Mankind has always remained in delusion about God-concept. As we have discussed in the earlier chapters' religion is deeply ingrained in the human mind. It is not possible to wipe out religious imprints. Individual psyche functions under the overawing influence of a religion. Religion may be any; it binds the mind to certain preordained drivers and influencers. A person practising any religion behaves encompassed within the religious parameters His behaviour, thinking etc., all remain impressed with the religious fervour he carries. We have discussed in the earlier chapters how man was confused over happenings outside his control, how he developed the concept of an ethereal power that supposedly controlled what was not within man's control. With so many concepts that man fabricated later, he got confused even more. The heavenly steam could not quench man's thirst to capture the abstract, he continues to roam in a desert looking for water in a mirage. In the history of religion's development man has stood at the crossroads many times and wondered which path to take. The confusion springs from the differing ideologies to which he was exposed. He takes a particular path getting over the confusion but enters a state of delusion as he is never sure if the chosen path will lead to emancipation. Even a crossover to another path does not eliminate his delusion. Confusion is a temporary state of mind, whereas delusion is a lasting mental state. One likes to harp on a belief but knows not for sure it to be true. Man does not know following a particular ritual will truthfully propitiate the supernatural power.

We must go to the basic reason for such confusion. Is there a God or no God? This question has engaged the human mind since antiquity without an answer. Vedic *rishis* were forthright in concluding that they did not know who to worship, how to worship, with what offerings. They expressed their misgiving in the *Hiranyagarbha Sukta* hymn of the universal womb. The opening lines translated tell us "In the beginning was the divinity in His splendour, manifested as the sole Lord of land, skies, water, space and that beneath and He upheld the earth and the heavens;: who is the deity we shall worship with our offerings?"[85]

Man did not know then nor knows now the nature of God, the Almighty. God has been conceived as either personal or impersonal. Western philosophers have classified the God-concept and coined different terms, like Theism, Deism, Polydeism, Autotheism, etc.[86] In theism, God is the creator as well as the sustainer of the universe, and revelations are an important part of theistic belief and knowledge. Whereas in Deism the God is the creator but not the sustainer. Deism is a philosophical position asserting that reason, and observation of the material world are sufficient to establish the existence of a Supreme Being, or creator of the universe and rejects revelations as the source of knowledge. Polydeism holds the belief that multiple gods exist, but do not intervene in the affairs of the universe. Autotheism is a belief that one has the ability to become godlike. Buddhism and Jainism are auto-theistic as they neither believe the existence of a creator god nor in the revelations. In pantheism, God is the universe itself. Atheism is an absence of belief in God, while agnosticism deems the existence of God unknown or unknowable. God has also been conceived as the source of all moral obligation, and the highest conceivable existence. Many notable philosophers have developed arguments for and against the existence of God.[87] Thus one can see that severe confusion reigns the human mind in so far as the concept of the supernatural power is concerned. It is ironical that mankind believes in the existence of a superpower but fights over man-made concepts, ideas and names! In the two centuries of crusades, Christian armies carried the True Cross expecting God to be on their side. Many battles were won but can anyone say that it was because God was on their side? Obviously no, since no such attestation can be asserted in the cases where the Christian armies lost to Muslim forces. The other explanation may be that the Christian or the Islamic God was more powerful in the crisscross battles. But then we are dividing the divinity which cannot be a universal truth. It is not possible to have two or many gods. Similarly, during the Islamic invasion in India, many Hindu worshippers may have been caught while they were worshipping. God could not protect them. So, in all such cases, whose side was God?

No one has seen any god-figure; it remains abstract in thought but casts indelible imprints on the mind. Unlike incremental scientific development, religious development has been chasmic with tectonic shifts. It has been a story where past beliefs were put to the test, criticised, and vilified. There has been a continuous effort to wean away people from past beliefs and force them to accept the newer belief. "Nothing is more usual and more natural for those who pretend to discover a new belief than to praises their own by decrying all others which have advanced before them."[88]

Many gods to one god concept was a cascading thought process resulting in one god concept. Zoroastrianism (5th Century BCE) perhaps was the first attempt to find a single god concept, the all-powerful Ahura Mazda, moving away from polytheistic concepts. However, in its development one can see clearly that in their concept of monotheism there was no fundamentalism. It did not decry other faiths. It mentions 'Other Ahuras' and also seeks benevolence of other gods like 'Oh! Vayu grant me this that I may smite the creation of *Angra Mainyu*—the evil part opposing *Ahura Mazda*.'[89] Even if some consider Zoroastrianism a monotheistic concept, the fact remains that they placed Ahura Mazda as the highest among other godly figures. It indicates that the Zoroastrian religion was not monotheistic in a real sense. It did not profess a creationist god. They believed in the higher and universal qualities of humankind. They advocated *Humata* (good thought), *Huxta* (good words), and *Huvarshta* (good deeds). Persian emperors following Zoroastrian religion were tolerant towards other religions, a fact born out of the history of successive Persian empires and its recorded societal culture. Zoroastrian religion flourished in Persia for about 1000 years from 600 BCE to 650 CE when the Sasanian Persian empire was overthrown and extirpated by the Muslim invasion.[90]

During the same period, or even before, polytheistic concept thrived in different parts of the world. Greeks worshipped many gods in a pantheon. So did the Sanatana Hindus in India which remains polytheistic to this day. Greek philosophers did worship a pantheon of gods, but they also conjured the idea of one god. Several Greek philosophers thought deeply about the concept of god, and taught the relevance but differed in the concept and approach. Religion tends to teach morality but Socrates (C 470-379 BCE) was tried and executed for impiety that he was trying to pollute the young minds of Athenians. He is considered as one of the founders of Western philosophy and teacher of morality but was executed ironically, for teaching morality! Morality against blind belief on religion and faith is always a superior human attribute. Ancient Greeks were a highly developed cultural society. It was natural for them to examine the most vexed question, what is God. For Xenophanes (C 570-475 BCE), "God is thought as the fundamental principle of the universe . . . everything in the Universe is God, and God is in everything in the Universe . . ."[91], a thought re-echoed centuries later by Baruch Spinoza—*Deus sive Natura,* essentially meaning that God and Nature are the same and interchangeable. While writing on the 'Nature of God' S.E. Frost wonders "Is God a person . . . or a name for the force or forces which has brought the universe into being and sustain it?"[92] Conceptually, the nature of God differs in each religion, principally because god-concept, its nature and attributes-form or formless abstract-is a product of the human mind. That is what prompted Xenophanes to say that the nature and feature of god would have been like a horse, or oxen, or a lion if these could paint like humans. "So, the Ethiopians make their gods black and snub-nosed, the Thracians give theirs red hair and blue eyes."[93]

The God-concept is woven around probabilities and chance deduction. It is difficult to say if a theological shift was a chance deduction or rational outcome. One does not know whether following a path will lead to the esoteric domain we call heaven, the Empire of God. In my opinion, this happens only because we all try to search for the abstract iconic figure or a non-iconic idea with the gross parameters. It is like chasing a shadow, a dream, outside the realm of the manifest world. That is why it is challenging to realise the Almighty. Moreover, He is not an icon or non-iconic figure; He is an idea, a concept. Even if considered a figure, His body is spread over the whole universe as the presence of Almighty, being transcendent and immanent, is in every speck of dust, animate and inanimate. The human mind cannot capture the image and see Him; it can only experience the divine. You do not see the cool breeze but certainly feel it! But man has always tried to see the figurative of the formless, basis of theism and deism!

Man's life is torn between two worlds, one, the terrestrial and the other, the esoteric; former is tangible to our senses whereas the latter is the incomprehensive part about which we can only procrastinate and guess. The human mind has been guessing about heaven and hell, and the afterlife since sapiens came into existence. Man cannot discard any, neither the material world nor the ethereal. The material world is what he lives in, feels, and sees objects as real, therefore cannot discard it. And cannot discard ethereal as man has always felt that there is a different world beyond the material world, and he needs to safeguard his afterlife. The mind remains engaged with the possibility of heaven and hell. Myth and reality are thus separate yet entwined—the myth of heavenly abode and reality of terrestrial life. Entrapped in between, the human mind remains confused about where to find the Absolute Truth. Is the world as our senses perceive the real world, or is there another world beyond, which we cannot perceive with our senses? It reminds one of chapter 11, of the Gita. When *Arjuna* declines to fight, Lord *Krishna* shows him the cosmic universe. The Lord endows *Arjuna* with celestial vision, without which the cosmic universe could not be seen (experienced). Is this world of ours a Maya as conceptualised and preached in Sanatana (Hindu) philosophy? Has the physical world evolved from a never changing Absolute or come about without a priori? Is this material world going to dissolve in the never-changing Absolute? Viewed from the standpoint of the material world, one sees change taking place continuously, but from the standpoint of the macrocosm, there is hardly any change. Take the example of a top. The peripheral lateral displacement will be much greater than at the bottom of the revolving pin. Similarly, lateral displacement at the periphery of the universe will be hugely greater than at the centre where there may not be any appreciable displacement. As you go deeper towards the centre of any object, including the universe, space shrinks, and Time accelerates. We appreciate day and night with earth's revolution at the periphery of the globe. But there may not be any diurnal change at the centre of the earth. Therefore, changes are relational. With all such thoughts, you may clearly see that the human mind can only conjecture and confabulate on the nature and feature of the Absolute. It remains beyond the grasp of the human mind. That is why knowing the Almighty is trying to know the unknowable!

Anyways you think the Almighty is beyond the material world. It is not possible to contain it within the doctrines of a religion. How can you arrest the infinity in words, a circle or a line? How can you define the undefinable? How can you confine the limitless in the binds of *naam-roop* (name and form)? One is reminded of the mythical story from the epic, Mahabharata, so beautifully described in poetic form by the famous Hindi poet Ramdhari Singh Dinkar in his book, *Rashmi Rathi,* where Lord Krishna goes to Duryodhana before the commencement of the battle to ask him for five villages in favour of Pandava so that war could be avoided. Duryodhana not only refuses but advances to arrest Lord Krishna who was an incarnation of Vishnu—a futile exercise indeed! Lord Krishna then attains his infinite posture and dares Duryodhana to bind the universe contained in Him. He mocks Duryodhana by asking him, "If he has brought big enough a chain to bind a billion galaxies, stars, and planets?" and then leaves the royal court declaring that now the war is inevitable. No religious binds can encapsulate the Almighty. In the effort to describe the nature and feature of the Almighty, man has created only confusion in his mind and continues to remain in the state of delusion.

So, what man can do to realise the Almighty? The simple answer is to love all that is in the material world considering it a reflection of the Almighty. Individual effort must be supportive of Nature and not exploitative. Rights and duties come side by side. Man's actions should be supportive of the divine wish if it believes the divinity to be the cause of the manifest world. Fundamental rights cannot be claimed while ignoring the fundamental duties. Mankind should take up the responsibility to care for and protect the domain of Almighty, which is the whole universe, all the sects, all the clans, all that is in nature, instead of nursing a parochial and sectarian outlook.

Therefore, a sectarian concept of god and the flawed concept that whatever is in the universe is for the use of mankind fails on logic. Spinoza holds, "God is identical with the universe and must be and act according to eternal and necessary laws."[94]

It may not be easy to comprehend such philosophical stand as one can always say that the eternal and universal law was also a product of God's mind, and being the author, He can always transgress his own created thoughts, limits, and fetters! But why should He? Only based on changing religious concepts conjured by the human mind. If it were so then, He would be changing His stance every now and then, and that cannot be true as we know that Almighty is one, is transcendental, and has remained the same, immutable. There has to be permanency in the non-changing concept of the Almighty. Material truth is temporary and transient like a living species which undergo fundamental change upon death. The macrocosm of creation is also transient and temporary. It is only the Almighty that is unchanging, hence the Absolute Truth! And it cannot keep changing.

However, humanity remains divided on monotheistic and polytheistic concepts. God in monotheistic thought is conceived as the Supreme Being, the creator with attributes being omnipotent, omnipresent, and omniscient. He is also supposed to be omnibenevolent. In other words, his benevolence is universal, showering on the whole world, the whole humanity. But in a contradiction, the monotheistic religions remain sectarian in their applicability and approach. Even though it may not be appreciated by those within monotheistic religions fold, viewed from outside it may appear confusing.

One may wonder as to how a religious sect, like Hindus, have so many gods. That, at first glance, appears a logical and legitimate inquiry. However, if you confabulate on the issue, you will realise that these iconic representations are based on the different human attributes. *Durga Saptshati* is a collection of hymns in the praise of Goddess Mother. Chapter 5 of *Durga Saptshati* specifically strikes with wonderful hymns relating to different human attributes. In fact, different deities represent and address different qualia of human mind. The deistic approach with karma doctrine in the polytheistic way of worship has a distinct advantage. For example, if a person suffers in poverty, perhaps goddess Lakshmi has not been benevolent on him, or if a person remains poor in studies, perhaps goddess Sarasvati has not been benign. If there is continuous unexplained suffering, it is the karma that may have played truant. Thus, there are outlets to explain away sufferings in the deistic and karmic concept without positing it on the Almighty. This is precisely why there is no concept of 'anti-god' in Hindu religion. Concept of *asura* or demons are there, but it does not stand opposed to the Almighty. In fact, they worship the same godly figures that a human being does. Absolute Truth in Hindu religious concept is not the deities, not even the trinity of Brahman, Vishnu, Mahesh, but a *Parabrhaman*—the attributeless, transcendental across epochs and, straddling beyond all description and conceptualisation. All sufferings are posited on different deities or one's karma, instead on the Almighty, thus, indemnifying the Almighty from negativity.

The Vedic seers wondered how creation came into being, and who was the creator? They were candid in accepting their ignorance. The ambiguity of creation is well expressed in *Nasadiya Sukta,* where Vedic seers wondered how creation came into being. Through *Hiranyagarbha Sukta*, they wondered about the identity of the deity, or an idea, one should worship! The ambiguity continued not only till the development of the concept of trinity in the form of Brahman, Vishnu, and Mahesh (the creator, preserver, and destroyer), conceptualised in the post-Vedic period, but even beyond. Religious syncretisation did not end there. Local deities were conceptualised, such as *gram devata*—a village deity, and *Kul devata*: a family deity, with symbolic representation. Hindus worship almost all objects, oceans, rivers, trees, stones, mountains, etc., as symbolic to the Almighty. This may tend to explain the presence of a pantheon in the Hindu Sanatana religion, but it does not satisfy the confusion or the delusion we all have in our mind, in fact, for some, in a superficial consideration it may further fortify it. Because in that case, one may wonder as to why worship a pantheon, why not he Supreme Being, the *Parabrahman?* The answer, perhaps, lies in the concept that the *Parabrahman* is conceived as being without attributes *(Nirguna)* where prayers cannot affect it either way. Offerings and obeisance will not stick, will make no dent on its equanimity—the subscribed nature of *Parabrahman*.

One view is that the Almighty controls every act, every change that takes place in the universe, and the other is that the universe, once having been borne is automated, and changes take place due to natural laws. It is natural that the universe expands; there is no hand pushing its boundaries. Earth revolves on its axis and around the sun due to natural laws of attraction and repulsion, no finger holds the pinion. Birth and death are a natural phenomenon. Growth from childhood to adult follows natural laws. Nature provides nutrition on certain natural principles. Of course, one may argue that everything is by the will of the Almighty, but scientific knowledge humanity has gathered through past millennia tells us differently with testable proofs. Moreover, if all happenings in the physical world are divine-ordained, no one stands to blame on wrongdoing; there may not be any necessity of confession. And there will be no incentive to human endeavour. However, the cosmic providence in the balanced non-chaotic universe, the support system for sustaining the living and non-living world, and the universal laws of nature cannot be refuted. One may not visualise the contribution of cosmic life energy, but then there is no other alternative to suggest; the divine contribution cannot be refuted. It can only be praised and marvelled!

At best, we may assume that the Almighty cast a body and breathed life into it. In other words, one may subsume that for Him, the task was creation of a living body and mind, and not their individual qualities. Then the divine work was half done, which again cannot be accepted so long we believe in the omniscience of the Almighty. But the same omniscience cannot produce sinners as that would be against the basic concept that the Almighty is all purity. Then who could be the maker of individual nature and mind? Let us assume that man himself is the builder of his mind and his own nature. Many will argue against, but the fact remains that terrestrial factors come into play in the mental construct. External factors such as the environment, the society, and nature are the contributing factors as discussed in the earlier chapters. A healthy body is a prerequisite of a healthy mind, and bodily health is dependent on many other factors, including the food intake of an individual. The mental health or mental attitude, similarly, is dependent on external factors, including the environment, as the mind is a developmental phenomenon. It appears that cosmos and living world are working in tandem; cosmos providing the basics of the manifest world and the living world sustaining life! Thus, the concept of deism appears logical and probable. But man continues to remain in delusion about the divine and anthropomorphic contribution.

4
I, Me, Myself

"Therefore, as it seems, it is the greatest of all disciplines to know oneself. For when a man knows himself, he knows God!"
— Clement of Alexandria

i. General Consideration

EACH INDIVIDUAL IS A UNIQUE ORGANISM AND DISPLAYS an independent aura. Most of our thought process and behaviour remains highly individualistic. The selfish attitude is the centre point that dictates our conduct. We cannot get out of the circle of I-ness. You can turn the pages of human history and see how rigid individualised thinking and beliefs, quite against logic and rationality, brought unimaginable suffering to humanity. Many politicians destroyed the political and social prospect of a developing country right at the birth of a nation. Their self-held beliefs overrode logic and rationality. Such leaders force their individualistic viewpoint. They manufacture arguments in support and carry their coterie along with. Many decisions they take may not be in the overall interest of the country, but they force it only to satisfy their ego.

They think they know everything, and what they do not know does not exist; whatever passes through their mind may be the last word, the gospel truth! Decisions may not be good for society or the country either in the short term or the long term, but they force it through silencing any dissent. Later events may show the illogicality, but they find an excuse in a scapegoat. In fact, it is quite well recorded in the world history of political development that many politicians at the helm have taken society on a disastrous path. And in order to establish a social order of their choice, they have upturned the social structure, many may have been uprooted, many lives lost, but they did not have any concern. They went along with their personalised view. Damage done to society is in direct proportion to the level they occupy in the political or administrative hierarchy. All possess a self-centric mind, be it a prime minister, or a commoner.

We are more concerned about how we appear to the outside world but only through the lens of the self-vision. Interaction between the external world and internal self is obsessively crucial for any person. By external world I mean all that is outside us, be it a person, society, or environment. Since a person forms an opinion from his emotions, his reading of another individual, or an issue, will keep changing in accordance with his emotional construct at that point in time. Love and hate, pleasure and pain are all feelings governed by the instant emotional construct in a person. It may undergo change as what one hates or despises today, he may love or like tomorrow, or *vice-versa*. The feeling and emotional reaction of different individuals on the same external cue will be different as the individual nature and emotional constructs are individualised and different in different persons. If a school student is doing well in his studies the felt outcome of a teacher and a classmate may be different. The teacher may praise him, reward him, whereas his classmate may develop a sense of envy, at times hate him. Therefore, what 'A' feels about an issue would be different than that of 'B'. It is a human nature that what one likes he wants to preserve and propagate, and what he dislikes he tries to ignore or destroy.

It takes many factors to develop an individualistic outlook, but if you watch the behaviour of a person, it would be evident. You will be able to catch their idiosyncrasies, peculiar habits, and individualised thinking. Also, every individual is judged by their outlook and attitude on different matters. Some have identified these as quotients: personal quotient (PQ), intelligence quotient (IQ), social quotient (SQ), and emotional quotient (EQ). All these help to determine the composite behavioural attitude of a person. Everyone understands what is meant by IQ. It is a commonly used term in psychiatric evaluation, and even in day-to-day discussions. SQ defines the social standing of an individual. Social standing stands firmly in the mind and heart of a person, rich or poor, a politician or a commoner. One fears the loss of face, meaning thereby a sharp fall in SQ in the eyes of the society. People are known to have entered into an altercation, arguments, aggressive and violent behaviour to protect their SQ. People do not bat an eyelid even committing murders to protect family honour. Emotional quotient is the scale of signifying control over emotions. People who commit suicide are low on EQ. They seem to have lost their capability to balance their emotions. Composite of SQ, IQ, and EQ is the PQ, that is the exhibited attitude and behaviour of a person to the external world. This exhibited attitude of a person is not fixed and keeps changing with time and place. One can also change his attitude with personal effort, education, logical and rational thinking, etc., to determine his social standing. In other words, it is possible to improve the personal quotient (PQ).

Everyone tries to learn about themselves, but some only achieve knowledge about the self. This is mainly due to the lack of objectivity because being objective to the self, howsoever rewarding, is difficult. Most of us are deliberately not objective, or we ignore objectivity for the sake of preserving self. We like to live in an ivory tower which we have allowed our subjective mind to create. Many fear that if they try to capture the true-self through objectivity, some embarrassing shadow may envelop this ivory tower of falsity which they have so untiringly preserved for self-aggrandisement. We also fear that our falsity will be exposed to our own superconscious, altering the false self-image and self-held beliefs. Therefore, we like the darkness to prevail. Such people fail to see the blissful radiance in the knowledge of the true self and illumined conscious awareness! And the true self is not what we perceive in the conscious awareness. Freud argued, ". . . we cannot equate the self with consciousness as our mental life . . . is governed by the unconscious a roiling cauldron of memories, associations, reflexes, motives, and drives."[95] In simple terms, it means that what we perceive about ourselves may not be a true reflection, as the overall behaviour and conduct are a result of internal disposition.

There is another important aspect, that is the factor of envy. Not only we feel envious of the success of other but also feel relieved having escaped suffering that another person may have faced. It is a natural tendency in everyday life. Spinoza puts it in the following words: ". . . Men generally rejoice as often as they recall past evils suffered by anyone, and why they delight to relate perils from which they have escaped.[96] The individual mind always compares events and people in day-to-day life. And in this way, one feels relieved that he did not suffer what another may have. One may say that this is a selfish feeling, but men are selfish. The humane reaction could have been a sense of empathy, but it is not common because our mind is deeply personalised.

There are different kinds of men in the world, and when we compare one with another, or with ourselves, we distinguish them mainly by their emotional mind, and exhibited behaviour. We tend to say A is egalitarian, B is superstitious, C is intrepid, some others are envious of my achievements etc. That is when we compare from the standpoint of personal ego. When God blessed Adam and Eve 'to be fruitful and multiply' and gave them dominion over 'all other living things'[97] the ego in man multiplied million times, and one started to hold the belief that he is the lord over nature. Whereas. Man being the highest of biological species on earth has a duty to preserve and nurse the godly dominion. Ironically, ego may be individualistic but is bolstered by society, by religious doctrines, myths, and parables. From ego rise desire, and other negative attributes, like envy, avarice, hatred, etc. Man hangs like a pendulum swinging perpetually between sin and virtue, always trying to reach the Escapement, (the mechanism which engineers the swing), to stop the swing, but failing in the attempt, time and again.

Each human being is interrelated. Even the strangers are interrelated. It is universal. Closer, the object greater is the pain and anguish. But the degree of pain will be in proportion to individual mental construct. In the words of Baruch Spinoza "... the pleasure and pain of one person differs only from the pleasure or pain of another in so far as the nature or essence of one differs the nature or essence of another."[98] So, it is the nature of the individual mind that determines the effect as pleasure or pain. Surely, many may have felt a pang just by the thought of someone getting hurt. The tinge I feel is peculiar; it always appears on the shin of the right leg and lasts only for a moment. Those who feel pain or anguish with even a thought of someone else getting hurt are significantly interconnected in comparison to those who may not be bothered. Similarly, if you listen to a musical note or a rendition that touches your heart, you develop Goosebumps. What is all this? Its pathophysiology is revealed on deeper contemplation. All these, an event, or a thought, create vibration, and some of these vibrations touch your heart. It travels to the mind and causes different effects, sometimes of pain, sometimes of awe, and sometimes of joy and happiness. Each such vibration tries to find imagery from within the collage of stored memory to relate. If a vibration matches a joyful memory of childhood, or nostalgic pine of teenage days, our mind tries to go back to that imagery and enjoy it as was enjoyed earlier. Of course, the intensity of the vibration cannot be the same being in a different 'time-space' frame. When our mind revisits a sorrowful moment or a period of grief, one feels negative vibrations, but the intensity reduces as imagery fades with time. That is why we say, "Time is the greatest healer." All such feelings are in the proportion to your emotional mind that determines its severity.

An individual is a mind-body complex. It is essential to understand that the psychological propensity of an individual is not static; it keeps changing. However, the basic template, the fundamental nature has a feature of constancy. Mostly, a person is selfish, sees things from the standpoint of individualised mind. The outcome in a self-centric mind (discussed next) will be in the perspective of subjectivity, and therefore, lack objective assessment.

ii. Self-Centricity

"The psyche is one of those things which people know least about because no one likes to inquire into his own shadow."

— C. G. Jung

From the above quotation, it appears Carl Jung must have penetrated the mind to have come to this conclusion. How accurate is the observation is quite remarkable. Majority of us do not want to look into our mind and see the shadow of our inner personality we possess and carry around. Firstly, it is not easy, and secondly, one feels it will bring out our lies and falsity which will be too embarrassing to confront! Men like to preserve individuality. It is a universal law of existence. But man being a social animal has to reckon with the interrelatedness in the world. Thus, there is a continuing battle between individuality and societal norms. It is like putting a test tube with liquid material in a centrifuge. Heavier molecules will settle at the bottom. When all interrelatedness is in the centrifuge of mind, self-centricity is the centrifuged result at the bottom and everything else is supernatant. The feature of self-centricity starts forming from childhood. A child always wants to be the centre of attraction. It starts when a child begins attracting his mother with cries, and later with his tantrums. It generates out of egocentricity or egocentrism. In the majority of cases, it gets balanced when a growing child confronts the world and acquires a sense of objectivity. However, some retain childhood self-centricity and remain subjective throughout their lives.

Most of us possess a self-centric mind. A self-centric person will always think only about himself or herself. They feel that the world should revolve around them. They generally feel at the centre of their immediate and extended surrounding. Their conduct in any family or social gathering is quite apparent. They like to talk continuously trying to draw attention and do not hesitate to intrude themselves in the middle of a discussion, even to the point of cutting off someone in the middle of a sentence. They talk more and listen less, a core feature of a self-centric person. This signifies their belief that anything and everything must happen where they are in the focus. They also enjoy putting someone down to derive pleasure out of it. If they catch you on a wrong foot (in their opinion), a self-centred person will not bat an eyelid to denounce and embarrass you even publicly. They rejoice having scored a point, but basically, it is their sense of envy that they nurse.

Principally, they are cynics as they like the outside happenings to take place as per their centricity which they know that cannot be true. thus, they despise occurrences and ideas outside their mental realm. They like to associate with cynics as that gives strength to their thoughts, and they feel their attitude reinforced. It may be stated here that negative minds attract negativity, and positive minds attract positivity, opposite to the accepted principle of magnetism in physics.

Most of us indulge in daydreaming. It is a positive attribute as it lets your mind wander into the rose-garden of probabilities. Daydreaming is future-focused but different from desire and hope. Desire and hope are what one aspires and consider achievable within the realm of individual capability, whereas daydreams are outside this realm unless made possible with the intervention of fate. Cynics with negative mind also indulge in daydreaming but usually reminisce the past to imagine a gloomy future.

A self-centric person also cannot imagine things happening without their intervention or accept something going wrong due to their actions. This way, their self-centric mind gets satiated. Self-centric persons are severely subjective, and whenever a thing goes wrong, they try to blame it on others, and sometimes even on fate or destiny but never on themselves. Another trait that can be found in self-centric people is that they exhibit bravado but feel insecure from inside. They also keep thinking that no other person recognises what goodness they possess, and keep reminiscing and tormenting themselves about it all the time.

There is yet another trait usually seen in self-centric people. If they do not find the expected response, their mind remains fixed and they keep coming back to the same point. Supposing they tell you to do something and you postpone it for a while for whatever reason. After some time when you return, you start talking about something else, such as dark clouds you saw when out on a stroll. You are immediately stopped and reminded of the matter which was the point before you went out. For them, the time had stayed at a fixed point in the meanwhile, and life started once again with the reminding of the topic. This is called 'fixation of idea'. Nothing can be more important for a self-centric person than the formatted idea in their mind.

However, self-centricity should not be confused with narcissism. They may appear synonymous, but there is a subtle difference. Narcissism is attachment to the body, whereas self-centricity is attachment to one's own mind. Self-centricity is egocentricity where a person is unable to differentiate between objective reality and subjective assessment. It is the inability to view a perspective through other than one's own mind.

Now let us look at the featured attributes of a self-centric in more detail. Usual attributes in a self-centric person are highlighted below:

1. Sense of Superiority:

A self-centric person views himself better than every other person. They feel they can never be wrong. In order to feel superior, they undermine other people's attributes and amplify their own attributes and achievements. But this feeling of superiority is false as the comparison has been selective. No one is the master of all trades. So, it may not be right to pick and compare between two individuals. But a self-centric mind has to satisfy a sense of superiority for its own sake, hence selects the areas where it finds itself proficient. Nothing deters a self-centric person; he or she will manufacture arguments, or find faults with others which favours their mentation.

2. Likes and Dislikes:

A self-centric person has strong likes and dislikes. It comes from the stand that there is nothing grey in their dictionary; everything is either black or white. If someone is right in their opinion, that person is good all the way and if not then that person is terrible all the way. Such a mindset leaves little choice with them. It is a well-known fact that any situation has multiple options and there are many ways to look at an object. But a self-centric person cannot see all the options and possibilities. For them, there is only one canvas, the canvas of good and bad! It is evident, therefore, that they discard the option to analyse a situation, a system, or an idea, objectively. Once having made up their mind, they cannot be dissuaded easily. They will not agree even if proven wrong and try to find justifications with motivated reasoning to suit and satisfy their preformed conclusions. Motivated reasoning is a phenomenon where people cull out and access arguments that favours a preconceived notion. They construct and evaluate arguments in a biased manner to endorse a preferred conclusion. Thus, they generally nurse subjectively biased preformed notions and create a dissonance in their mind. People know that in a discussion, one may win or lose, but a self-centric person always likes to win regardless whether their arguments are logical and objective or not.

3. Insecure and Vulnerable:

A self-centric personality primarily is insecure and vulnerable. Such a mindset arises from the constant need to prove themselves the best in their preferred fields. . It is needless to say that such an attitude is false as they also know that they may not be the best in every scenario. But to satisfy their egoistic nature, they consider themselves better than others. And since they put themselves at a higher platform, they always feel insecure about losing their pre-eminence as has been manufactured by their self-centric mind. They consider the outside world a threat to their beliefs and ideas and therefore, feel vulnerable. For them, the outside world is envious and always in search of attacking their self-held beliefs. In their heart of heart, they know the falsity, but they prefer to live in a world of make-belief.

4. Like-Minded Circle:

From the insecurity and vulnerability arises the quest to have like-minded people to interact. That is why a self-centric will try to gather people around who display a liking for them. However, they never try to gather like-minded self-centric people around, as that would obviously lead to a conflict as each will have a self-centric worldview of their own. But their effort is to gather people who are supportive and accept their individualistic attitude and superiority and generally be in agreement with the central figure. Therefore, their social circle can never be significantly large

5. Lack of Empathy:

Generally, a self-centric person has a deep attachment with the self. The sense of attachment extends to their offspring and shows in their outward behaviour. It is natural to love your children, but for some, it becomes a passionate behaviour with an undue sense of attachment. They display little concern and have little empathy for others. They nurse deep attachment to persons who they like, have branded them as good people, close relatives, etc. They feel nursing and showing empathy to others may reduce the quantum of love and affection they would like to preserve to shower on the liked and closely attached. However, such personalised feelings are baseless, as love and affection do not reduce even when showered upon others. It is not a money bank account that dwindles as you spend, but a vault of abstracts that does not follow any arithmetical formula.

6. Sense of Possessiveness:

Carl Jung maintains that "There are, unfortunately, many parents who [like to] keep their children infantile because they do not wish to grow old and give up their parental authority and power."[99] The reverse is equally true when a son or a daughter continues to have a strong attachment with parents. It too hampers a healthy personality development. The parental authority and exercise of parental power must gradually end when the child grows to be an adult. In many instances, it does not happen. Some parents like to continue to exercise undue control over their children, forgetting that their child has grown into an adult now and is free to pursue his or her own life. He or she may have his or her own ambitions, dreams to pursue, and societal obligations (an adult is a unit of society) just like his parents. Some parents try to showcase the achievements of their children without the knowledge of their children, even when they are adults and pursuing a successful career. Their aim is to tell others how well their property (the child) has done well in a competitive world. You market a product only when you think you are the owner of the product. So, the sense of ownership extends from the feeling of owning your body to your children. Such an attitude is clearly a by-product of a sense of under confidence, an underlying trait of a self-centric mind.

7. Focus More on Superficial:

A self-centric person has little interest in other's work. They pick out another person's behaviour only what suites to their way of thinking and working. The rest does not have any value for them. They fear that if they like other's work, it may rob them of self-held belief of singularity and superiority. They are merely disinterested and are indifferent to other's ideas. Their indifference is not for the different qualities of another person but on the person as a whole. They are generally critical of others. They are not interested in another person's hobby or vocation, even if the person is usually held in high esteem by the public at large. Thus, it is evident that they are more interested in the superficial instead of the inherent qualities of another person. They are generally, blind to their own faults but very alive to the errors or mistakes of others, and do not lose an opportunity to point out other's shortcomings.

8. Self-Opinionated:

A self-centric person is highly self opinionated. They have their ideas or their own take on every matter. The opinion of others has little value for them, howsoever logical it may be. They resent others who do not agree with them. For them, everyone else must like or hate the object on the same scale, and to the same degree, as they do. Obviously, this is not possible since the mental perception and the level of likeness or dislike will be different in different people.

Some Tips to Deal with a Self-centric Person:

These are the usual traits found in a self-centric person. It has been described differently by different experts, but the gist is what has been stated above. The bottom line is that it is not difficult to identify a self-centric personality, but dealing with them is difficult and requires immense forbearance and patience. The question arises that how can one deal with a self-centric person. One can find many suggestions or prescriptions in scientific papers, books, and on the internet, but there is no easy solution. The main reason for it being that the facile ability of a self-centred person is to 'shoot and scoot'. They listen to you only to the extent it suits their way of thinking. The moment they feel the arguments are likely to rob them of their self-held beliefs, they simply break away from the conversation or change the track. However, the below-mentioned tips may be of some help:

1. Listen carefully to whatever they say. Do not let them feel that you are inattentive. The moment they think you are not paying the expected attention; their mind will start alienating and dissociating.

2. Be flexible to whatever they suggest, even if it is against your basic comforts and convenience.
3. Whatever you may not agree upon, just ignore it. When confronted with such a situation, just get away from the scene, if not physically then at least mentally. Also, do not argue in order to prove a point to such a person.
4. Self-centric people like to provoke to start an argument. Do not fall in the trap. Just ignore it. However, if there is a possibility to reach an amicable discussion, do enter the argument, but conclude it quickly. The more you extend the argument the more are the chances of getting into an unsettled bitter ending. So, try to avoid it.
5. If you have a hobby nurse it and remain immersed in it as much as you can, if you do not have a hobby, develop one apart from the domestic chore and the usual routine.
6. Make them feel happy as much as your inner personality will generally accept. It may be a temporary solution because, through these kinds of acts, you may not be able to change the fundamental mindset of a self-centric person. So even if it works temporarily, it could help you circumvent any unpleasant situations.

As I said earlier, there is no easy solution as self-centrism is a psychophysiological state of mind which is difficult to change. But the following from Mother Teresa encapsulates how to deal with such people, "People are unreasonable, irrational, and self-centred. Forgive them anyway."

5
In Conclusion

"Knowledge can be communicated, but not wisdom. One can find it, live it, be fortified by it, do wonders through it, but one cannot communicate and teach it."
—Hermann Hesse

It is natural that a person who has travelled widely will know the world much more than you and me. Knowledge about the world for an Indian village person may be limited to the 25-mile radius, but his worldly knowledge may not be limited to the 25-mile radius. He may be as wise, or perhaps wiser as he may know himself, nurse lesser degree of ego, envy, and sense of superiority. An illiterate villager may have better common sense than a well-educated, well-travelled person. Therefore, only knowledge does not create wisdom. It is your analytic mind that imparts wisdom. In knowing the 'self', a person has to apply his understanding, his wisdom, not only his knowledge.

Philosophers and thinkers have tried to work out how our mind works. They have tried to understand how thought, emotion, and consciousness are interconnected? How can one formulate a conjunction theory between thoughts and the mind? How the mind fits into the rest of the material world.? The Mind has the capacity to cognise sense perceptions but does it have the capability to see beyond? These are some questions that have agitated philosophers and thinkers from ancient times. Neither science nor metaphysics has a clear answer. The abstractness of the mind continues to remain an enigma. It is difficult to chart out the process of the mental construct in an individual because there are many factors involved, such as the surroundings, the environment, etc. And, most importantly, the developing mind itself. At every stage of development, our mind acquires some peculiarity, which influences further mental development, adding another bead in the string of conscious awareness. The individual ego, the I-ness are the dominant factors influencing mental development. Therefore, the mind is the sculptor as well as the product. Ego is a helper, as well as an obstruction in the realisation of the self. Ego is a helper, since without ego, one will not be able to identify oneself. And, without identifying himself, he can never realise the 'self', because there will be no object to objectify. Ego is an obstruction, as well, since it conditions the mind to individualism, without obtaining an objective outlook, and realistic worldview. The fundamental characteristic of a human being is a normal state of awareness formulated by science and society. There are two aspects, one is the surrounding world, and the other is the individuality. By the term 'individuality' I do not mean an individual but a person with all the attributes acquired during individuation.

A drop of ink in an ocean becomes invisible but retains its tiny presence in all the parts of the oceanic water. The same is true when one dissolves his tiny ego in the sea of cosmic consciousness. The ink of individual ego becomes invisible, though remains there in a minute proportion. It does not get extirpated. That tiny drop comes face to face with the human mind. Its imprint is present all the while in our consciousness. Unless one dissolves this 'tiny ego' in the cosmic consciousness, it will resolutely bind the individual mind, and make the self-realisation difficult.

Religion casts a deep impression on the individual mind and is a significant influencer in the development of a personality. Humanity has experienced the shifting rainbow colours of religion since the beginning. In the search for an ideal religion, man has just been extricating itself from one quicksand to another, from one quagmire to another, achieving nothing more than fracas, dogma, religious wars, and conflicts. It is well-known that finding an ideal religion may not be easy due to man's ego, and ego in man is not going to evaporate. The only way one can escape from the religious cage is by inculcating spirituality from within.

Religion and spirituality are at two different planes. One may be irreligious but be spiritually inclined. The first step towards spirituality is to let go of your egoism. Many believe that it is possible to subdue your ego completely. I do not think it is possible to extirpate the ego within you completely. Even if you achieve such a state, it will be meaningless. Because without the identity of self, what may be the usefulness of attaining a spiritual plane? Yes, one can always subdue self-ego, and all the associated features, like desire, avarice, envy, anger, hatred, etc., but should not fall in the trap of destroying self-identity by completely destroying self-ego, as that would mean destroying the self-esteem.

Life is mysterious. Scientists and philosophers have been trying to unravel the mystery of life, but a clear hypothesis is yet to emerge. Within the anatomical body, there exists an energy body which departs from a dying person. Rarely, it returns energising its mind. On recovery, such a person may remember the experience as out-of-body or near-death experience.

How and why bodily growth takes place in a particular fashion is a marvel we can only wonder. How different parts of our body develop from single-cell biology, and how each part of the body functions and takes shape in a particular manner is mind-boggling. Just look at the musculoskeletal, the excretory, the reproductive systems etc., in a human body. All these put highly developed science with profound discoveries and ideas to shame. The human mind, with all its intelligence, is unable to decipher the preformed formulae in an embryo. What records does it carry from the previous generation(s) and what, how, and why it records events of the present life has eluded the human understanding, so far. Science has discovered many aspects of the genes, its characteristics, and tinkered with the genome system trying to breed ideal human being, but a clear picture of the peculiar development of the human mind is not yet known. Genetic engineering is already a developed science and widely practised in agri-products. But experimenting with mankind has met with resistance mainly due to ethical consideration, and perhaps due to the fear of improbability of the unpredictable results.

Even the basic as to how the mind-brain complex works to convert thoughts and ideas into action and feelings, and how does it retain sense perceptions etc., is not yet clearly known. Scientists and philosophers continue to confabulate and develop hypotheses but are yet to discover the connecting bond between the mind and the brain. Scientists of biology and medicine believe that the mind does not have a separate entity; it is a part of the brain. However, many argue to the contrary, and the debate continues. Memory is the most critical attribute of the mind. Our actions, and at times, inaction is retained in the mental vault as good and bad memories.

Not only one needs to look within, but the external factors are also crucial in the process of knowing the self. One has to be objective and critical of the external factors as well. Unless you cognise the external environment objectively, you may run into the misty clouds of falsity. That may make things difficult in knowing the self. If you are in a position of power and get a lot of attention from your social circle, you have to examine it objectively. Otherwise, you may take it to be the truth, whereas reality may be quite different. Flattering only raises the egotism in a person, not a good contribution to knowing the self. In the knowing of the self, one has to be severely objective and critical of himself, and his mind. He must discover ontology and epistemology of his action, the 'why' part, not only the 'how' part. What we observe is relative to our mental frame and emotional construct at that particular time and space, and most importantly, the ratio of subjectivity and objectivity. Each of us possesses the ability to evaluate our actions, our thoughts. The problem is that we mostly remain encapsulated within the influencing sphere of subjectivity. Our objective mind should continuously evaluate our thoughts, and our actions, using the SWOT analysis-strength, weakness, opportunities, and threat.

There are two groups of human behaviour, one that revolves around the self, the centripetal, and another which moves away from the centre of the person. These two groups largely determine the overall bias in an individual. The ego reinforces the centripetal, whereas spirituality is the centrifugal force trying to pull away from the centre-point-ego. Scientists have tried to compute human behavioural attributes in a mathematical formula to peep into and understand a mental state. They have aggregated good and bad qualities of the human mind separately and tried to convert these into numerical calibration to compare what is good and what is not good. Ego, avarice, greed, anger, and hatred are on the negative side, and empathy, forgiveness, etc., are on the positive side. Then, they have tried to find an equation to describe the mental attitude of a person to determine his overall personality. How far it helps, one does not know, but the work of a renowned psychiatrist and philosopher, David R. Hawkins (1927-2012) in this regard has been remarkable. He says, "Man is stuck with his lack of knowledge about himself until he can learn to look beyond apparent causes."[100] Unfortunately, most of us remain entwined in the vineyard of apparent causes and fail to see the underlying roots through which causes arise, and thus fail to realise the true nature of an effect. Whenever an external idea strikes, your mind starts to compare it on the scale of your individualised thinking. Whereas objectivity demands real-time assessment and evaluation. A painting is appreciated on its inherent qualities, what it depicts, and what it conveys, not only on how it appears. Objects must be valued on its own, objectively, and not through the prism of subjectivity!

Each individual looks for glorification through self-aggrandisement. We want to be everything we come across in our day-to-day life. When we read a novel, we wish to be the character we liked the best. However, the selection is not on the merit of the character, but upon our subjective mental make-up. When we watch a romantic scene in a movie, we want to replace the hero or the heroine with ourselves. When we listen to an inspiring speech, we want to be the speaker. We want to do all these little realising that the reality is different than what our subjective mind gathers. Howsoever we want, we cannot walk into a virtual garden and pluck a flower for real. The problem is that we examine things with a subjective mind, not on the scale of objectivity.

Researching on the topic has been a great journey. I have experienced changes in myself during the period. It is not only the knowledge I have gathered, but the whole experience has been of great value. I can say with confidence and certitude that my ego, self-centricity, my arrogance (at whatever level possessed earlier), and the individualism in me, all have changed to a balance between imagination and reality.

I consider it a positive development. Life is experiential, and the learning process lasts till death. An event, a particular episode, or a period of confabulation leads to a different state of awakening. That is the positive result of the learning process. I hope the readers may experience the same as me, only then I will consider having contributed my bit on this contentious subject of knowing the self! And please note that knowing the self is highly important to see the entire picture. As Osho (1931-1990), popularly known as Bhagwan Rajneesh says, "Man is not a question, but a quest. A question can be solved intellectually, but a quest can only be solved existentially."[101]

Acknowledgements

Researching and writing this book has been a great journey. It may not have been possible without the support of many. It is my pleasure to acknowledge the support and prompt response I received all the time from the IIC library staff and in particular Hema, Rajiv and Shefali.

I posted some excerpts on Facebook as I progressed while completing the manuscript and received excellent positive responses from friends, colleagues, and relatives. It made me confidently realise my usefulness. Post-retirement, many feel of little value and relevance. Therefore, a feeling of relevance naturally is rewarding and invigorating. I believe that post-retirement, life is another phase. It is *vanaprastha* as per the Hindu philosophy. You wander in the *Aranyaka* (the forest), initially aimless but feel the eternal joy in finding an aim, a tradition to follow. While wandering in the forest of mentation, I immersed myself in the love for literature and writing, which has not stopped since. The stream has not dried up.

The best part of this phase of life is that you can choose what you want to do and what you want to pursue. There is no binding and no cellar-walls to prevent the sunshine. You are free from performing any assigned task and free to choose your own path. I am thankful for this phase in my life; perhaps it has been more rewarding intellectually than the active service I had with the Air Force. But that is not to say that the Air Force service was of no consequence. It will be a grave folly to ignore the contribution of a brilliant phase in my life. The experiences gained were of immense value in my literary pursuit. I am thankful to the Indian Air Force for enhancing values of life, the support I received, and keep receiving even to this day!

I regularly interacted with my previous publishers, Kalpana Shukla of K. W. Publishers, Kunal Marathe of erstwhile 'Author's Empire' and Karunesh Agrawal of Cyberwit Publishers, and thank them for their supportive stance and encouragement.

I cannot ignore the support I received from my friends and colleagues. Especially from my Air Force buddy, Gautam Guha, who has been a continuous source of encouragement. My intellectual discussions with Gurcharan Das, a prolific writer and a well-renowned author, added to my intellectual bank. I am thankful to him. I had regular poetic and literary interaction with Late Dr H. K. Kaul who was the president of the Poetry Society of India. Regrettably, he died recently of Covid-19 infection leaving a huge gap in the literary circle and Library Sciences of which he was the father-figure in India. May his soul rest in peace. I will miss him.

In the era of IT, who can remain without the use of the Internet? It is a vast library of knowledge where you find almost anything you want to. There are many, but I found Wikipedia the most useful and most user-friendly. Millions visit this site is every day. If they wanted, they could have garnered lots of advertisements, but they have desisted from the attractive financial gain only for the sake of remaining purely academic. I, for one, do sometimes contribute financially, as I feel such endeavours must be supported. There are other portals also, but I use Wikipedia regularly. I am thankful to all the internet sites and portals for what they stand for and the knowledge they disburse.

Of course, I am thankful to Hay House publishers for approving my submission promptly, within a short time and especially Ruchita Ahuja and Rajalakshmi for open-minded and frank discussions, and Aditya Jarial who so professionally edited the manuscript and made valuable suggestions to improve upon. A manuscript is the raw material and editing is to polish it to an end product.

Last but not least, I must profusely thank my wife, Usha, for letting me concentrate on my writing. She, in her own way, kept me relieved of many tasks that provided me with ample time to reflect, research, and write.

References

1. Chakrabarti, Kisor Kumar, *Classical Indian Philosophy of Mind*, State University of New York Press (1999), P-6.
2. Jung, C. G., *Psychology and Religion: West and East*, Tr. by R. F. C. Hull. Routledge (1969), P-486.
3. Jung, C. G., *Civilization in Transition*, Tr. R. F. C. Hull, (First published 1964, this Reprint 1970), P-249.
4. Ratner, Joseph. *The Philosophy of Spinoza*. Modern Library (1927), P-149.
5. Spinoza, Baruch. *Spinoza's Ethics*, Tr. Andrew Boyle, Everyman's Library, (This last Reprint, 1970), P-35.
6. Jung, C. G., *Collected Works, Vol VII*, Second Edition, Tr. R. F. C. Hull, Routledge (1968), P-147.
7. Jung, C. G., *Collected Works, Vol VII*, Second Edition, Tr. R. F. C. Hull, P-19 and 28.
8. Dostoevsky, F., *The Brothers Karamazov*, Kindle Edition, Loc-2239.
9. htts://en.wikipedia.org/wiki/Silbo_Gomero. Accessed on October 14, 2019.
10. Descartes, Rene, *Meditations on First Philosophy*, Kindle Edition, Loc-983-988. Accessed on March 30, 2020.
11. Aristotle—Wikipedia _the Soul. Accessed April 01, 2020.
12. https://en.wikipedia.org/wiki/Ensoulment. Accessed on September 14, 2019.
13. Ibid.

14. https://www.ncbi.nlm.nih.gov/pmc/articles/PMC3616796. Accessed on September 14, 2019.
15. Russell, Bertrand, *A History of Western Philosophy,* Simon and Schuster, Thirteenth Printing (1959), P-5
16. Unitarianism—Wikipedia. Accessed on December 10, 2020.
17. Ibid.
18. Pruthi Harb, *Hijackers of Faith*, self-published, (2009).
19. Swami Vivekananda, Vedanta, *Voice of Freedom*, (Ed) Swami Chetanananda, Advaita Ashram (1987), P-85.
20. Ibid, P-77.
21. Swami Rama, *Spirituality: Transformation Within and Without*, Kindle Edition, P-38. Accessed on Jun 25, 2020.
22. Frawley, David, *What Is Hinduism?*, Bloomsbury (2019), Kindle Edition, Loc-587. Accessed on May 20, 2020.
23. Greenblatt Stephen, *The Rise and Fall of Adam and Eve*, The Bodley Head, London (2017), P-49.
24. Noah, Harari Yuval, *Sapiens: A Brief History of Mankind*, Kindle Edition, Location 3254. Accessed on May 10, 2020.
25. Venkataraman, Iyer, M. K., *Advaita Vedanta*, Asia Publishing House (1964), P-22.
26. Schrodinger, Erwin, *What Is Life?*, Kindle Edition, P-126. Accessed on June 16, 2020.
27. http://www.bbc.co.uk/religion/religions/atheism/types/buddhistatheism.html. Accessed on June 13, 2018.
28. Ratner, Joseph, *The Philosophy of Spinoza*, Random House. Modern Library (1927), P-1.
29. Krishnamurthy, V., *Essentials of Hinduism*, Narosa Publishing House (1989), P-51.
30. Russell, Bertrand, *A History of Western Philosophy*, Simon and Schuster, New York, Thirteenth Printing (1959), P-xiv.
31. Dostoyevsky, F., *The Brothers Karamazov*, Kindle Edition, Loc-5175.

32. *Vedanta: The Voice of Freedom*, (Ed) Swami Chetanananda, Advaita Ashram (1987), P-83.
33. https://en.wikipedia.org/wiki/Opium_of_the_people. Accessed December 21, 2020.
34. Heehs, Peter, *Spirituality Without God*, Kindle Edition, Loc-248. Accessed on April 10, 2020.
35. https://en.wikipedia.org/wiki/Spiritual_but_not_religious#cite_note-Nones_on_the_Rise-14. Quoting from Funk, Cary; Smith, Greg, '"Nones" on the Rise: One-in-Five Adults Have No Religious Affiliation'.
36. Venkataraman, Iyer, M. K., *Advaita Vedanta*, Asia Publishing House (1964), P-65.
37. Swami Rama, *Spirituality: Transformation Within and Without*, Himalayan Institute Press, 1988, Kindle Edition, P-4.
38. Punja, Shobhita, *Divine Ecstasy: The Story of Khajuraho*, Penguin (1992), P-87 and 88.
39. Ibid, P-90.
40. Mukherjee, S., *The Gene: An Intimate History*, Kindle Edition, P-22. Accessed on April 09, 2020.
41. https://en.wikipedia.org/wiki/Charaka and https://en.wikipedia.org/wiki/History_of_genetics. Accessed on April 10, 2020.
42. Mukherjee, S., *The Gene: An Intimate History*, Kindle Edition, P-46 and 47. Accessed on April 09, 2020. https://en.wikipedia.org/wiki/Hugo_de_Vries.
43. https://en.wikipedia.org/wiki/Eugenics. Accessed on May 08, 2020.
44. Basham, A. L., *The Wonder That Was India*, third revised edition (paperback), Sidgwick & Jackson, First Published 1954, This First Paperback Edition (1985), P-270.
45. Chakrabarti, Kisor Kumar, *Classical Indian Philosophy of Mind*, State University Press, New York (1999), P-132 and 133.

46. Russell, Bertrand, *A History of Western Philosophy*, 1945, P-134.
47. Hawkins, David, *The Eye of I*, Kindle edition, Page-59. Accessed on June 02, 2020.
48. Gordon, Jesse E., *Personality and Behaviour*, McMillan (1963), P-176.
49. https://en.wikipedia.org/wiki/Cognition. Accessed on April 13, 2020.
50. *Spinoza's Ethics*, Tr. Andrew Boyle. Every Man's Library, First published (1910), This Reprint (1970), P-37.
51. Krishnamurthy, V., *Essentials of Hinduism*, Narosa Publishing House (1989), P-61.
52. https://en.wikipedia.org/wiki/Mind%E2%80%93body_problem. Accessed on June 20, 2020.
53. Arendt, J., *Melatonin and the Mammalian Pineal Gland*, Edition 1, London Chapman & Hall, 1995, P-17. As mentioned at https://en.wikipedia.org/wiki/Pineal_gland#cite_note-13. Accessed on October 15, 2019.
54. https://en.wikipedia.org/wiki/Galen. Accessed on October 10, 2019.
55. https://link.springer.com/article/10.1007/s00381-015-2636-3. Accessed on January 25, 2020.
56. https://quotefancy.com/quote/11150/Nikola-Tesla-If-you-want-to-find-the-secrets-of-the-universe-think-in-terms-of-energy. Accessed on April 15, 2020.
57. Swami Sivananda, *Mind: Its Mysteries and Control*, The Divine Life Society (1974), P-5.
58. Chakrabarti, Kisor Kumar, *Classical Indian Philosophy of Mind*, State University of New York Press (1999), P-182.
59. Chakrabarti, Kisor Kumar, *Classical Indian Philosophy of Mind*, State University of New York Press (1999), P-16.
60. Ibid, P-116.

61. Venkataraman, Iyer, M. K., *Advaita Vedanta*, Asia Publishing House (1964), P-6.
62. https://www.brainyquote.com/quotes/galileo_galilei_161381. Accessed on October 10, 2019.
63. Smith, Anthony, *The Mind*, Hodder and Stoughton (1984), P-4.
64. Ibid, P-29.
65. Smith, Anthony, *The Mind*, Hodder and Stoughton (1984), P-97.
66. Hampshire, Stuart, *Spinoza and Spinozism*, Oxford University Press (2005), P-91. Accessed on May 17, 2020.
67. www.verywellmind.com. Accessed on April 22, 2020.
68. Jung, C. G., Lecture delivered on October 19, 1936, 'The Concept of the Collective Unconscious' to the Abernethian Society at St. Bartholomew's Hospital in London.
69. Jung, C. G., *The Archetypes and the Collective Unconscious*, Tr. R. F. C. Hull, Routledge (1968) II Edition, P-3.
70. https://www.verywellmind.com/what-are-jungs-4-major-archetypes-2795439. Accessed on April 17, 2020.
71. John Locke—Wikipedia.
72. Humphreys, Christmas, *Karma and Rebirth*, John Murray, London (1943, This Reprint 1959), P-17.
73. Radhakrishnan, S., *Indian Philosophy*, McMillan (1927, Eighth Impression, 1958), P-25.
74. Osho (Bhagwan Rajneesh), *Intuition: Knowing Beyond Logic*, St. Martin Griffin, New York (1976, Reprinted 2001), P-10.
75. https://en.wikipedia.org/wiki/Intuition. Accessed on November 05, 2019.
76. Ibid.
77. Hume, David, *A Treatise of Human Nature*, Oxford University Press, First Edition (1888), This Reprint (1967), P-67.

78. Alexander, Eben-Newell, Karren, *Living in a Mindful Universe*, Kindle Edition, P-22. Accessed on May 12, 2020.
79. 'Raja Janak: Was that true or this is tue?'—Aman Bedi Astrology.
80. https://en.wikipedia.org/wiki/Psychoactive_drug, quoting from the work of Merlin, M. D. (2003), 'Archaeological Evidence for the Tradition of Psychoactive Plant Use in the Old World'. Accessed on December 01, 2019.
81. https://en.wikipedia.org/wiki/Psychoactive_drug, quoting from https://www.bbc.com/news/science-environment-11878241. Accessed on December 01, 2019.
82. News item, Times of India (Bangalore edition), November 23, 2019.
83. Jung, C. G., *Collected Works*, Tr. R. F. C. Hull, Vol 11, 'Psychology and Religion West and East', Routledge, P-519.
84. Jung, C. G., *The Collected Works of C. G. Jung*, Vol 17, 'The Development of Personality', Tr. by R. F. C. Hull, Routledge, London (First printed in 1954, Reprint 1994), P-51 and 52.
85. Hiranyagarbha—Wikipedia.
86. God—Wikipedia.
87. God—Wikipedia.
88. Hume, David, *A Treatise of Human Nature*, Oxford, first published in 1888, Reprint 1967, P-1.
89. https://en.wikipedia.org/wiki/Zoroastrianism. Accessed on April 28, 2020.
90. Ibid.
91. Frost, S.E., *The Basic Teachings of the Great Philosophers*, Blackiston, Reprinted 1945, P-11.
92. Ibid, P-109.
93. Ibid, P 112.

94. Spinoza, Baruch, *The Philosophy of Spinoza*, Copyright by Modern Library Inc. (1927) with Introduction by Joseph Ratner of Columbia University Press, P-33.
95. Ramachandran, V. S., *The Tell-Tale Brain*, Windmill Books (2012), P-249.
96. Spinoza, Baruch, *Spinoza's Ethics*, Tr. Andrew Boyle, Everyman's Library (Reprint, 1970), P-116.
97. Old Testament (King James Version), Genesis, 1.28.
98. Spinoza, Baruch, *Spinoza's Ethics*, Tr. Andrew Boyle, Everyman's Library (Reprint, 1970), P-125.
99. Jung, C. G., *The Collected Works*, 'The Development of Personality', Tr. by R. F. C. Hull, Routledge, London (First printed in 1954, Reprint-1994), P-55.
100. Hawkins, David, R., *Power Vs Force*, Hay House Inc., Kindle Edition (Sample), Loc-532. Accessed on June 5, 2020.
101. https://www.facebook.com/osho.international/photos/new-series-playing-this-week-on-osho-radioosho-talks-about-sufism-and-takes-some/10155107918777069/. Accessed on September 02, 2019.

Internet Sources:

https://www.facebook.com/osho.international/photos/new-series-playing-this-week-on-osho-radioosho-talks-about-sufism-and-takes-some/10155107918777069

https://en.wikipedia.org/wiki/On_the_Soul

https://en.wikipedia.org/wiki/Ensoulment

Ibid

https://www.ncbi.nlm.nih.gov/pmc/articles/PMC3616796/

https://en.wikipedia.org/wiki/Upanishads

http://www.bbc.co.uk/religion/religions/atheism/types/buddhistatheism.shtml.

https://en.wikipedia.org/wiki/Opium_of_the_people

https://en.wikipedia.org/wiki/Spiritual_but_not_religious#cite_note-Nones_on_the_Rise-

https://en.wikipedia.org/wiki/Hugo_de_Vries

https://en.wikipedia.org/wiki/Charaka

https://en.wikipedia.org/wiki/History_of_genetics

https://en.wikipedia.org/wiki/Eugenics

https://en.wikipedia.org/wiki/Mind%E2%80%93body_problem

https://en.wikipedia.org/wiki/Cognition

https://en.wikipedia.org/wiki/Mind%E2%80%93body_problem

https://quotefancy.com/quote/11150/Nikola-Tesla-If-you-want-to-find-the-secrets-of-the-universe-think-in-terms-of-energy

https://en.wikipedia.org/wiki/Silbo_Gomero

https://www.brainyquote.com/quotes/galileo_galilei_161381

https://en.wikipedia.org/wiki/Pineal_gland

https://en.wikipedia.org/wiki/Galen

https://link.springer.com/article/10.1007/s00381-015-2636-3.

www.verywellmind.com

https://www.verywellmind.com/what-are-jungs-4-major-archetypes-2795439

https://en.wikipedia.org/wiki/Intuition

https://en.wikipedia.org/wiki/Psychoactive_drug

https://en.wikipedia.org/wiki/Psychoactive_drug

https://en.wikipedia.org/wiki/Zoroastrianism

Bibliography and Further Reading

Classical Indian Philosophy of Mind. Chakrabarti, Kisor Kumar. State University of New York Press (1999).

The Master Key System. Charles, F. Haanel. Kindle Edition (2014).

Psychology and Religion: West and East. Jung, C. G. Tr. R. F. C. Hull, Routledge (Reprint 1969).

Civilization in Transition. Jung, C. G. Tr. R. F. C. Hull, (Reprint 1970).

The Philosophy of Spinoza. Ratner, Joseph. Modern Library (1927).

Spinoza's Ethics. Spinoza, Baruch. Tr. Andrew Boyle, Everyman's Library (Reprint 1970).

C. G. Jung, Collected Works, Vol VII, Second Edition. Tr. R. F. C. Hull, Routledge (1968).

Mind: Its Mysteries and Control. Sivananda, Sri Swami. The Divine Life Society (1974).

The Development of Personality. Jung, C. G. The Collected Works, Tr. R. F. C. Hull, Routledge (Reprint 1994).

The Brothers Karamazov. Dostoyevsky, F. Rupa Publications (2013), Kindle Edition.

A History of God. Armstrong, Karen. Vintage Books (1994), Kindle Edition.

Meditations on First Philosophy. Descartes, Rene. Kindle Edition.

Hijackers of Faith. Pruthi Harb. Self-Published, (2009).

Spirituality: Transformation Within and Without. Swami Rama. Kindle Edition.

The Story of Svetketu. Goenka, Shri Vincent Shaw., Kindle Edition.

What is Hinduism. Frawley, David. Bloomsbury (2019), Kindle Edition.

The Rise and Fall of Adam and Eve. Greenblatt, Stephen. The Bodley Head, London (2017).

The Philosophy of Spinoza. Ratner, Joseph. Random House. Modern Library (1927).

Essentials of Hinduism. Krishnamurthy, V. Narosa Publishing House (1989).

Spirituality Without God. Heehs, Peter. (Bloomsbury), Kindle edition.

The Holy Bible, Samuel 15:3 (New International Version), Deuteronomy 20:13-14, & Numbers 15:35.

The Voice of Freedom. Vedanta: (Ed) Swami Chetanananda, Advaita Ashram (1987).

A History of Western Philosophy. Russell, Bertrand. Simon and Schuster, New York, Thirteenth Printing (1959).

Psychology and Religion: West and East. Jung, C. G. Tr. R. F. C. Hull, Routledge (Reprint 1991).

Sapiens: A Brief History of Mankind. Noah, Harari Yuval. Kindle Edition.

Advaita Vedanta. Venkataraman, Iyer, M. K. Asia Publishing House (1964).

Spirituality Without God. Heehs, Peter. Kindle Edition.

Spirituality: Transformation Within and Without. Swami Rama. Himalayan Institute Press, Kindle edition (1988).

The Gene: An Intimate History. Mukherjee, S. Kindle Edition.

The Wonder That Was India. Basham, A. L. Third revised edition (paperback), Sidgwick and Jackson (1985).

A History of Western Philosophy. Russell, Bertrand. Simon and Schuster (1945).

The Eye of I. Hawkins, David. Hay House, Kindle edition (2001).

Personality and Behavior. Jesse, E. McMillan (1963).

Spinoza's Ethics. Tr. Boyle, Andrew. Everyman's Library, Reprint (1970).

Mind: Its Mysteries and Control. Swami Sivananda. The Divine Life Society (1974).

Essentials of Hinduism. Krishnamurthy, V. Narosa Publishing House (1989).

Mindfulness the Master Key. Swami Chaitanya Keerti. Wisdom Tree, New Delhi (2016).

Ethics. Spinoza, Benedict de. Tr. R. H. M. Elwes. Kindle Edition.

Jung, C. G. Collected Work, Vol 9, Part II, Second Edition. Tr. R. F. C. Hull, Routledge (1968).

The Mind. Smith, Anthony. Hodder and Stoughton (1984).

Spinoza and Spinozism. Hampshire, Stuart. Oxford University Press (2005).

'The Concept of the Collective Unconscious'. Jung, C. G. Lecture delivered on October 19, 1936, to the Abernethian Society at St. Bartholomew's Hospital in London.

The Archetypes and the Collective Unconscious. Jung, C. G. Tr. R. F. C. Hull, Routledge (1968).

Psychology and Religion West and East. Jung, C. G. Tr. R. F. C. Hull, Collected Works, Vol 11, Routledge.

Indian Philosophy. Radhakrishnan, S. McMillan, Eighth Impression (1958).

Intuition: Knowing Beyond Logic. Osho (Bhagwan Rajneesh). St. Martin Griffin, New York, Reprint (2001).

A Treatise of Human Nature. Hume, David. Oxford University Press, Reprint (1967).

Living in a Mindful Universe. Alexander, Eben—Newell, Karren. Kindle edition (2017).

Divine Ecstasy: The Story of Khajuraho. Punja, Shobhita. Penguin (1992).

The Development of Personality. Jung, C. G. Reprint (1994).

The Basic Teachings of the Great Philosophers. Frost, S.E. Blackiston, Reprint (1945).

Hegel's History of Philosophy, New Interpretations. Ed. David A. Duquette. State University of New York Press (2003).

The Philosophy of Spinoza. Spinoza, Baruch. Introduction by Joseph Ratner of Columbia University (1927).

Personality Assessment. Semeonoff, Boris. Penguin Books (1966).

What is Life? Schrodinger, Erwin. Kindle Edition, Reprint (2013).

Power Vs Force. Hawkins, David, R. Hay House Inc., Kindle Edition (2012).

Notes

1. Aldous Huxley (1894–1963): He was an English writer, philosopher, and a prominent member of the Huxley family. He is best known for his novel, *Brave New World*, set in a dystopian London. Source: en.wikipedia.org.
2. Aristotle (384–322 BC): He was a Greek philosopher and scientist who graduated from the Plato's Academy in Athens and was the tutor of Alexander the Great.
3. Aurobindo Ghosh (1872–1950): Born in Calcutta (now Kolkata), he was educated in England and is the founder of Shri Aurobindo Ashram in Pondicherry (now Puducherry).
4. Baruch Spinoza (1632–1677): He was a Dutch philosopher who argued that God is nothing but nature or the force of nature. He was excommunicated for his controversial views through a *cherem* (Jewish Fatwa).
5. Helena Blavatsky (1831–1891): Born into an aristocratic Russian-German family, she was an occultist, spirit medium, and author who co-founded the Theosophical Society in 1875 in New York City. She started her spiritual quest in her childhood and travelled widely, including to India. Her theosophical doctrines influenced the spread of Hindu and Buddhist ideas in the West.

6. Carl Gustav Jung (1875–1961): He was a Swiss psychiatrist who founded Analytic Psychology. A prolific writer not only in psychiatry but in many other fields, such as philosophy, religious studies, and archaeology. Jung created some of the best-known psychological concepts, including the archetype, the collective unconscious, the complex, and extraversion and introversion.
7. Charles F. Haanel (1866–1949): He was a noted American philosopher and businessman and is best known for his contributions to the New Thought Movement through his book, *The Master Key System.*
8. Cob Mathew: He is a professor of Zoology at the University of Manchester and a member of Life Science Research Themes—Computational and Evolutionary Biology.
9. Charles Darwin (1809–1882): He was an English naturalist and geologist, and is best known for propounding the evolutionary theory. He established that all species of life have descended over time from common ancestors and evolution resulted from natural selection.
10. Erwin Schrödinger (1887-1961): He was a Nobel-prize winning Austrian physicist who developed a number of fundamental results in the field of quantum theory, which formed the basis of wave mechanics.
11. Epicurus (341–270 BC): He was an ancient Greek philosopher and the founder of the school of philosophy called Epicureanism. He taught that pleasure and pain are measures of what is good and evil and death is the end of both body and soul, and should therefore not be feared.

12. David Hume (1711–1776): He was a Scottish philosopher, historian, economist, and essayist who is best known for his highly influential system of radical philosophical empiricism, scepticism, and naturalism.
13. H. G. Wells (1866–1946): He was a prolific English writer in many genres, including history, politics, and social commentary. His most notable science fiction work is *The Time Machine*.
14. Thomas Hobbes (1588–1679): He was an English philosopher and is best known today for his work on political philosophy.
15. Immanuel Kant (1724–1804): He was a German philosopher and argued that fundamental concepts structure human experience, and that reason is the source of morality. His beliefs continue to have a major influence on contemporary philosophy, especially the in fields of metaphysics, ethics, political theory, and aesthetics.
16. Gottfried Wilhelm von Leibniz (1646–1716): He was a German polymath and philosopher, and to this day, he occupies a prominent place in the fields of mathematics and philosophy.
17. John Locke (1632–1704): He was an English philosopher and physician and is regarded as one of the most influential of Enlightenment thinkers. He is also known as the 'Father of Classical Liberalism'.
18. Nicholas Roerich (1874–1947): He was a painter, writer, archaeologist, theosophist, philosopher, and public figure, who in his youth was influenced by the occult. He was interested in hypnosis and other spiritual

practices and his paintings are said to have hypnotic expression. Born in Saint Petersburg, Russia, to a family of a well-to-do notary public, he lived in various places around the world until his death in Naggar, Himachal Pradesh, India.

19. Osho (1931–1990), also known as Acharya Rajneesh, and later, Bhagwan Shree Rajneesh, was an Indian mystic, guru, and spiritual teacher. His international following has continued even after his death.

20. Plato (428/427 or 424/423–348/347 BC): He was an ancient Greek philosopher and mathematician. He founded the Academy in Athens, the first institution of higher learning in the Western world. Along with his teacher Socrates and his most famous student, Aristotle, he laid the foundations of Western philosophy and science.

21. Ramakrishna (1836–1886): Born Gadadhar Chatterji/Chattopadhyay, he was an Indian mystic and yogi during the 19th-century. His religious school of thought led to the formation of the Ramakrishna school by his chief disciple, Swami Vivekananda.

22. Radhakrishnan (1888–1975): He was an Indian philosopher and statesman who was the first vice-president of India and the second president of India. One of India's most distinguished twentieth-century scholars of comparative religion and philosophy, his academic appointments included the King George V Chair of Mental and Moral Science at the University of Calcutta and Spalding Professor of Eastern Religion and Ethics at Oxford University.

23. Rene Descartes (1596–1650): He was a French philosopher, mathematician, and scientist who

spent most of his life in the Dutch Republic. He has been dubbed as the father of modern philosophy. His best known philosophical statement is 'Cogito ergo sum'.

24. Sigmund Freud (1856–1939): He was an Austrian neurologist and is known as the father of psychoanalysis. Freud's redefinition of sexuality to include its infantile forms and led him to formulate the Oedipus. He also postulated the existence of libido, an energy which generates erotic attachments and neurotic guilt. In his later work, Freud developed a wide-ranging interpretation and critique of religion and culture.
25. Socrates (470/469–399 BC): He was a classical Greek (Athenian) philosopher and is credited as one of the founders of Western philosophy. Plato and Xenophon were his two celebrated pupils. He was charged with corrupting the mind of the young generation of Athens and not acknowledging the gods of the city-state. He was tried and sentenced to death by drinking hemlock.
26. S. E. Frost Jr (1899–1978): He was a faculty at the Department of Education, Brooklyn College, New York. He spent many years in the study and teaching of the history and philosophy of education and is an author of a number of books on philosophy, religion, and education.

Index

Advaita: 48, 109, 116
Animism: 47, 55, 57
Baruch Spinoza: 16, 63, 106, 125, 163, 167, 176-177
Bertrand Russell: 64, 95
Bhuddhism: 49, 57, 61, 139, 161
Brahman: 39, 45, 81, 81, 109, 168-169
Carl Jung: 15, 17-18, 46, 124, 167-127, 137, 139, 156, 158, 179, 185
Christianity: 39, 56-59
Dualism: 99, 108-109
Epigenetic: 20, 89, 91, 93-94
Eugenics: 88-89
Hinduism: 30, 39, 43, 49, 52-53, 57, 86
Islam: 31, 38-39, 43, 46, 49, 53, 56-59, 65, 86, 139
Jainism: 30, 49, 57, 61, 161
Judaism: 31, 38, 49, 53, 57-58
Karma: 38-39, 87-88, 115, 168
Kosha: 28-29
Moksha: 39, 146-148
Monotheism: 53, 56-59, 62, 162
Osho: 139, 195
Pineal Gland: 108, 110-112
Polytheism: 55, 57-59
Prakriti: 25, 40, 46, 109, 115
Purusha: 25, 40, 46, 109, 115
Rene Descartes: 29-30, 34, 108, 111, 137
Sanatana: 31, 49, 52, 102, 163, 165, 169
Sigmund Freud: 126, 127, 139, 176
The Buddha: 61, 77, 147
Zoroastrian: 56, 162